What a blessing that we now have, in a new edition, the writings of Bl. Michael Sopocko, St. Faustina's principal confessor and spiritual director. What a light they shine on the significance of the Divine Mercy revelations and devotion!

— Ralph Martin, STD
Director of Graduate Theology Programs
in the New Evangelization
Sacred Heart Major Seminary
Archdiocese of Detroit

This is a very timely and important book.

Why do I say that? Because God entrusted so much into the hands of Bl. Fr. Michael Sopocko. God gave Bl. Sopocko a vocation to the priesthood. God gave him spiritual stewardship of the soul of St. Faustina Kowalska. God gave him the responsibility of carrying on the mission of St. Faustina, of taking the baton from her and continuing to run the race through the dangers of World War II, into the wilderness of persecution and exile, facing the challenge of the ban on the Divine Mercy message and devotion, and dying before that ban was lifted by Pope St. Paul VI in 1978.

God entrusted a lot to Bl. Sopocko!

Through it all, he remained a humble servant of Divine Mercy, of Christ and Christ's Church. And because of his faithful service, the Divine Mercy message and devotion has reached the entire world.

This book is a summary, a brief statement of Bl. Sopocko's theology of Divine Mercy, something critical for our times. Enriched by Dr. Robert Stackpole's expert commentary, this is a true Divine Mercy classic. Many of our Marian Helpers have wished for Bl. Sopocko's writings and wisdom to come back into print. Now, their prayers have been answered.

May you be as blessed by Bl. Sopocko's faithful wisdom as St. Faustina was!

— Very Rev. Chris Alar, MIC
Director, Association of Marian Helpers
Author, *Understanding Divine Mercy*

GOD'S
AMAZING
MERCY

Meditations by St. Faustina's
Confessor and Spiritual Director

Blessed Michael Sopocko, STD

Edited with Commentary by Robert Stackpole, STD
Director, John Paul II Institute of Divine Mercy

Available from:
Marian Helpers Center
Stockbridge, MA 01263
Prayerline: 1-800-804-3823
Orderline: 1-800-462-7426
Websites: TheDivineMercy.org
Marian.org

Library of Congress Catalog Number: 2022946418
ISBN: 978-1-59614-574-0
Publisher: Marian Press
Publication date: January 31, 2023

Imprimi Potest
Very Rev. Kazimierz Chwalek, MIC
Provincial Superior
The Blessed Virgin Mary, Mother of Mercy Province
June 29, 2022

Nihil Obstat
Censor Deputatus
June 29, 2022

This edition of *God is Mercy* by Bl. Michael Sopocko is an edited and anno-
tated version of the 1965 Marian Press edition, *God is Mercy: Meditations on
God's most consoling attribute* by Michael Sopocko, STD, translated from the
Polish by the Marian Fathers.

Excerpt(s) from *Walking with God through Pain and Suffering* by Timothy
Keller, copyright © 2013 by Timothy Keller. Used by permission of Dutton, an
imprint of Penguin Publishing Group, a division of Penguin Random House
LLC. All rights reserved.

Excerpt from *The Problem of Pain* by C.S. Lewis © copyright C.S. Lewis Pte
Ltd 1940. Reprinted with permission.

The cover shows Bl. Sopocko abiding in the center of the merciful Heart of
Christ, the rays of the Divine Mercy Image flowing through Bl. Sopocko out
upon the readers and the world.

Table of Contents

For Jim Anderson

"I thank my God upon every remembrance of you …
for your fellowship in the gospel from
the first day until now" (Phil 1:3-5).

"A PRIEST AFTER MY OWN HEART": THE LIFE AND MISSION OF BL. MICHAEL SOPOCKO

How does our Lord fashion a holy priest "after His own Heart"? He purifies that priest in the refiner's fire of suffering and tribulation, so that his suffering and his pure, self-sacrificial love resemble our Lord's own. Moreover, He brings that priest into close contact with other souls who are growing in holiness themselves, so that they enrich each other's faith and inspire each other's love for Christ.

Think of those many saints down through history who have encouraged and aided each other along the path to Heaven: St. Francis and St. Clare; St. Monica, St. Ambrose, and St. Augustine; St. Margaret Mary and St. Claude de la Colombière; St. Teresa of Avila and St. John of the Cross. We often think of St. Faustina's spiritual director, Fr. Michael Sopocko, as merely the primary witness of her sanctity, and, perhaps, as the agent that God used to arrange the painting of the Image of the Divine Mercy. But he was so much more than that! He was a true guide for her soul, and a man of enormous wisdom and courage — so much so that the Church beatified him in 2008. Indeed, he was a man of sanctity in his own right — a sanctity forged in the fires of trials and tribulations, as well as through his close relationship with St. Faustina. He was also a great Divine Mercy theologian, and the principal instrument that our Lord used to spread the devotion to the Divine Mercy to the ends of the earth. Jesus Himself revealed all this one day to St. Faustina, as she recorded in her *Diary*:

> Reverend Father Sopocko left this morning. When I was steeped in a prayer of thanksgiving for the great grace that I had received from God; namely, that of seeing Father, I became united in a special way with the Lord who said to me, *he is a priest*

after My own Heart; **his efforts are pleasing to Me. You see, My daughter, that My will must be done and that which I had promised you, I shall do. Through him I spread comfort to suffering and careworn souls. Through him it pleased Me to proclaim the worship of My mercy. And through this work of mercy more souls will come close to Me than otherwise would have, even if he had kept giving absolution day and night for the rest of his life, because by so doing, he would have labored only for as long as he lived; whereas, thanks to this work of mercy, he will be laboring till the end of the world** (*Diary*, 1256).

Michael Sopocko was born in what is now Lithuania in 1888 into a noble family, but one that had fallen into poverty. They worked out in the fields, and barely scraped together enough to survive. Yet they were a deeply devout Catholic family, as well. Young Michael was especially pious; he even built in the family home a little altar that he would use to help him pray. Not surprisingly for such a boy, he sensed within his heart a call to the priesthood when he was just 10 years old. It was only through the generosity of the rector of the seminary in Vilnius, however, that Michael was able to study there for four years for the priesthood, and that he was finally ordained in 1914, right at the start of the First World War.

At his first assignment as a parish priest in the small town of Taboryszki, Fr. Sopocko became active in the field of education, and attempted to open new schools for children in the war-torn rural villages in his area. Unfortunately, the authorities of the German army who gained control of Lithuania gradually tightened their restrictions on his activities, and eventually he was forced to leave.

In 1918, Fr. Sopocko sought to study for a degree in theology in Poland at the University of Warsaw, but illness and the worsening situation of World War I forced him to delay. A year later, he signed up as a military chaplain, serving the

Polish army in a field hospital during the conflict with Russia. After only a month, however, he asked to be sent to the front lines to serve the soldiers who were in the thick of the fighting. In addition to saying Mass for them, hearing confessions, and anointing the dying, he often found himself called on to organize better care for the wounded.

After contracting a very serious illness himself (typhoid fever, which almost cost him his life), he was posted to a training camp for military officers, where his talks on religious and patriotic themes were so highly regarded that they were published by the Ministry of Defense and used for instructing cadets in all military units. He also did his best to resume his theological studies, and he organized the founding of a school for orphaned children from military families. In 1924, Fr. Sopocko received the equivalent of a master's degree in theology, with a thesis on the deleterious effects of alcoholism on school-age youth.

The Bishop of Vilnius at the time recognized Fr. Sopocko's academic brilliance and pastoral zeal and appointed him director of military chaplaincies for the entire Vilnius region, with responsibility for the pastoral care of more than 10,000 soldiers. At about the same time, Fr. Sopocko was working to complete his doctorate in theology, and later he carried on with post-doctoral research. From 1927 to 1928, he also served as spiritual director of the seminary in Vilnius, and head of the pastoral theology department at Stephan Batory University (now Vilnius University) — extra duties that were so time-consuming that they ultimately caused him to withdraw from military chaplaincy work in 1929.

In all this, what do we see in Fr. Michael Sopocko? Our Lord had fashioned him by poverty and hardship into a character of extraordinary toughness, perseverance, and courage, as well as great compassion for the suffering. Although he was not aware of it at the time, he would need all these virtues in abundance when he was appointed in 1932 to be the usual confessor to the convent of the Sisters of Our Lady of Mercy in Vilnius. There, of course, he encountered a most extraordinary holy soul and visionary, Sr. Maria Faustina Kowalska.

It was actually in the Sacrament of Reconciliation that he first met Sr. Faustina, a very humble nun who was carrying a tremendous weight on her shoulders. The Lord had begun revealing to her His message of Divine Mercy — an urgent message that He wanted her to share with the entire world. But no one would believe her, not even her superiors in the convent, nor any of her regular confessors, save one: Fr. Joseph Andrasz, SJ.

Sister Faustina, therefore, had prayed to the Merciful Jesus for a spiritual director, someone who would help her and guide her, on an ongoing basis, to discern and do His will. Father Michael Sopocko was the answer to her prayers, and eventually he became the main promoter of her revelations. It was primarily through him that she would answer the Lord's call to spread Divine Mercy throughout the world. Saint Faustina wrote in her *Diary*:

> I asked Jesus to give these graces to someone else, because I did not know how to make use of them and was only wasting them. "Jesus, have mercy on me; do not entrust such great things to me, as You see that I am a bit of dust and completely inept."
>
> But the goodness of Jesus is infinite; He had promised me visible help here on earth, and a little while later I received it in Vilnius, in the person of Father Sopocko. I had already known him before coming to Vilnius, thanks to an interior vision. One day I saw him in our chapel between the altar and the confessional and suddenly heard a voice in my soul say, **This is the visible help for you on earth. He will help you carry out My will on earth** (*Diary*, 53).

Some of the readers of this book will already know the story of Fr. Michael's dealings with Sr. Faustina: how he tested, encouraged, and guided her in the years that followed. One of the principal biographers of Fr. Sopocko, Bishop Henryk Ciereszko, auxiliary bishop of Bialystok, summed up the first stage of his relationship with Sr. Faustina like this:

> In his own diary, Fr. Sopocko admits that, when Sr. Faustina told him the truth about Divine Mercy, she inspired him to research, study, and contemplate this mystery. At the same time, he also confessed that he was unable to properly understand what Sr. Faustina told him about her interior experiences and what the work that God had entrusted to her meant in the beginning. For this reason, he listened to her more closely, pondered what she said, studied, sought the counsel of others, and, only after a few years, understood the greatness and value of the truth about God's mercy for the Christian life as well as the importance of spreading this message to the entire world.[1]

At Sr. Faustina's insistence, Fr. Sopocko commissioned a painting of the Image of the Merciful Jesus, and he directed her to write down all that was happening in her relationship with Jesus Christ, which she recorded in her *Diary*. He also supervised the printing of the first copies of the Divine Mercy Chaplet, Novena, and prayers, as well as litanies that he himself arranged (including the litany that lies behind the chapter headings of this book), based on the words and phrases that Jesus had spoken to St. Faustina.

Sister Faustina wrote about Fr. Sopocko several times in her *Diary*, including statements about him made by Jesus Himself that she recorded. For example, as we have already seen, in entry 1256 Jesus said to her: **"He [Fr. Sopocko] is a priest after My own Heart; his efforts are pleasing to Me. ... Through him it pleased Me to proclaim the worship of My mercy."** In entry 86, Jesus said: **"Write that My eyes rest on him day and night."** In entry 1408 Jesus said: **"His thought**

---

[1] Bishop Henryk Ciereszko, "Blessed Michael Sopocko: The Apostle of Divine Mercy," *Rocznik Teologii Katolickiej*, tom XVII/2, rok 2018, p. 9.

is closely united with Mine, so be at peace about what concerns My work. I will not let him make a mistake." Such
extraordinary statements from Jesus were not only a divine
confirmation to Sr. Faustina that she could put her complete
trust in Fr. Sopocko's spiritual guidance, but also a prophecy
of the tremendous role that his efforts and writings would
play in the spread of the Divine Mercy message and devotion
throughout the world in the decades to follow. In entry 1390,
St. Faustina herself stated: "As a result of his efforts, a new light
will shine in the Church of God for the consolation of souls."

Even before Sr. Faustina's death in 1938, Fr. Sopocko
worked tirelessly to research and make the case for the establishment of the Feast of the Divine Mercy. For example, in
1936, he approached the Polish bishops with a request that
the Feast of Divine Mercy be established, and he contacted
the Primate of Poland, Cardinal Hlond, about this issue, as
well. In 1939, he went to Rome to share his views on this
matter. Nevertheless, these early efforts served only to
increase his awareness that it was necessary properly to prepare the soil before planting the seeds, so to speak, in order
that ecclesial support for the establishment of the Feast of
Divine Mercy could grow and flourish. As a result, he turned
his efforts to publishing articles about Divine Mercy in the
Liturgy in order to awaken in the People of God a desire for
this feast. And these efforts rapidly bore fruit; after reading
about devotion to Divine Mercy, many of the faithful began
to request that such a feast be established. Father Sopocko
then renewed his efforts to convince the bishops of Poland
to petition the Holy See for the feast, which (eventually) they
did. In the end, it was his scholarly efforts that served as the
basis for the ecclesiastical approval of the establishment of
the Feast of Divine Mercy for the whole Catholic Church in
our time.

Father Sopocko also never lost an opportunity to preach
about God's merciful love. For example, during Lenten devo-
tions, his homilies on Divine Mercy in Vilnius Cathedral drew
huge crowds from all over the city.

During the early years of the Second World War he also assisted the Jews in Vilnius, both spiritually and materially, to help them survive Nazi persecution. As a result, he found himself in increasing danger of reprisal, and at one time was even incarcerated by the Gestapo for several days while they investigated his activities. In March, 1942, the Nazis began to round up all the priests in Vilnius for deportation to concentration camps. Warned in advance by his housekeeper that the Gestapo had laid a trap to capture him in his apartment, he fled for refuge to an Ursuline convent, where the sisters sheltered him as he remained in hiding. For two years, he worked on the property as a gardener and carpenter under the assumed name Waclaw Rodziewicz.

In 1944, as pressure on Vilnius from the war subsided, Fr. Sopocko returned to his duties at the seminary, but it was not long before persecution began again: this time from the Communist leaders of Lithuania. They ultimately forced him to leave the country altogether, and in 1947 he relocated to Bialystok, in Poland. In that region, he helped to establish a new religious order (following many of the guidelines given by St. Faustina in her *Diary*), an order he had originally founded in the Vilnius region. The members are now known as the Sisters of the Merciful Jesus. He also resumed teaching, this time at the local seminary in Bialystok.

Father Sopocko's main concern, however, was the spread of the message of and devotion to the Divine Mercy, and to this cause he dedicated most of the rest of his life. As he wrote in his own journal: "[S]preading the message of Divine Mercy and the entire devotion among others ... is and will remain the driving force of my life, supported by the endless Mercy of God."[2] Bishop Ciereszko explains that Fr. Sopocko's total dedication to the spread of Divine Mercy was rooted not only in what he had learned from St. Faustina, but also in his own personal experience as a priestly shepherd of souls:

---

[2] Cited in *The Memoirs of Blessed Fr. Michael Sopocko* (Dublin: Divine Mercy Publications, 2017), p. 200.

As he came to recognize the significance of the truth about Divine Mercy in pastoral ministry, Fr. Sopocko — in his own intuition and devotion to pastoral ministry — noticed that the Divine Mercy apostolate and pastoral care are interdependent and connected in many ways. If the essence of pastoral ministry is to lead people to God, then what more can turn people to God than the truth that God is merciful? What more can change man than worshipping God in His mercy and imitating Him by performing works of mercy? In fact, as Fr. Sopocko stated, he himself began to discover how this truth had a beneficial influence on the faithful, especially those who experienced their own misery, weakness, and sin. As he witnessed how people converted; how their lives of faith deepened; and how their hope and trust in God strengthened, Fr. Sopocko became more and more convinced that teaching about Divine Mercy was very fruitful. In this way, it became clear to him that both pastoral ministry and the Divine Mercy apostolate are inextricably linked.[3]

Meanwhile, the bitterness of persecution continued to be a feature of the life of Fr. Sopocko, although it increasingly took the form of opposition from *within* the Church to his efforts to promote the Divine Mercy message and devotion. Sister Faustina prophetically foresaw that this would happen, and reflected upon it in prayer, as recorded in her *Diary*:

> One day, I saw interiorly how much my confessor would have to suffer: friends will desert you while everyone will rise up against you and your physical strength will diminish. I saw you as a bunch of grapes chosen by the Lord and thrown into the press of suffering. Your soul, Father, will at times be filled with doubts about this work and about me.

---

[3] Cpiereszko, "Blessed Michael Sopocko," p. 11.

I saw that God Himself seemed to be opposing [him], and I asked the Lord why He was acting in this way toward him, as though He were placing obstacles in the way of his doing what He Himself had asked him to do. And the Lord said, **I am acting thus with him to give testimony that this work is Mine. Tell him not to fear anything; My gaze is on him day and night. There will be as many crowns to form his crown as there will be souls saved by this work. It is not for the success of a work, but for the suffering that I give reward** (*Diary*, 90).

It seems that part of our Lord's intention in permitting Fr. Sopocko to face so much opposition was that he had to experience for himself how the grace of God's merciful love can carry us through all seemingly insuperable obstacles, and all kinds of suffering. Only in this way could he truly be inspired to devote the rest of his life, and all his energies, to preaching and promoting Divine Mercy. As Bishop Ciereszko puts it, Fr. Sopocko had to discover for himself, not just in theory, but in living personal experience, "the truth about the need for Christians to turn to God's mercy in their own spiritual and religious lives. There is no other way to explain his fervor in promoting this idea and devoting himself to this work."[4]

At the same time, Fr. Sopocko did not neglect to use the full capacity of his intellect in the service of God's merciful love. After all, he was a highly trained and brilliant theologian, and he pondered deeply the message of mercy proclaimed throughout Holy Scripture, and in the Church's theological tradition, especially in the writings of St. Thomas Aquinas. From 1959 to 1962, therefore, as a fruit of decades of research and reflection, he published a four volume magnum opus titled *The Mercy of God in His Works*, a comprehensive study of the theme of Divine Mercy in Scripture and in theology. (It was subsequently translated into and published both in French and English.)

---

[4] Ibid., p. 10.

In 1958, Fr. Sopocko suffered damage to a facial nerve that made it difficult for him to give public talks to large audiences, and in 1962 he was injured in a car accident, as well — all of which made it necessary for him to retire from most of his teaching and priestly duties. But he certainly did not retire from his zeal for promotion of the Divine Mercy message and devotion. From 1959 onward, however, he suffered an even heavier cross than these physical ones: namely, the temporary decision of the Holy See, based on a faulty translation of Sr. Faustina's *Diary* into Italian, to put a ban on the message and devotion in the forms proposed by her, a ban that would last 20 years (and would not be lifted until three years after Fr. Sopocko's death). Still, he never lost hope that the Church authorities would change their minds, and he was encouraged when an official investigation into Sr. Faustina's life and virtues was started in 1965 under the oversight of the young Archbishop of Krakow, Karol Wojtyla (the future Pope St. John Paul II).

Father Sopocko also comforted himself with the knowledge that St. Faustina had foreseen such seemingly insurmountable obstacles back in 1935, and had prophesied that these would not prevail over the mission they both had been given by the Merciful Jesus:

> Once as I was talking with my spiritual director, I had an interior vision — quicker than lightning — of his soul in great suffering, in such agony that God touches very few souls with such fire. The suffering arises from this work. There will come a time when this work, which God is demanding so very much, will be as though utterly undone. And then God will act with great power, which will give evidence of its authenticity. It will be a new splendor for the Church, although it has been dormant in it from long ago. That God is infinitely merciful, no one can deny. He desires everyone to know this before He comes again as Judge. He wants souls to come to know Him first as King of Mercy. When this

triumph comes, we shall already have entered the new life in which there is no suffering. But before this, your soul [addressing Fr. Sopocko] will be surfeited with bitterness at the sight of the destruction of your efforts. However, this will only appear to be so, because what God has once decided upon, He does not change. But although this destruction will be such only in outward appearance, the suffering will be real. When will this happen? I do not know. How long will it last? I do not know. But God has promised a great grace especially to you and to all those ... **who will proclaim My great mercy. I shall protect them Myself at the hour of death as my own glory** (*Diary*, 378).

As if to console him for the seeming failure of many of his efforts, in 1972 he was named an honorary Canon of the Chapter of the Metropolitan Basilica of Bialystok, although he was already near the end of his life. The hierarchy had temporarily rejected his mission to promote the Image, the Feast, and the Chaplet of Divine Mercy, and the supernatural revelations given to the world through St. Faustina, but it had not fully rejected him as a priest; on the contrary, he was known and loved by many as a courageous and loyal son of the Church.

Father Michael Sopocko died in his simple bedroom in Bialystok on February 15, 1975, providentially on the day of the commemoration of St. Faustinus, the patron saint of Sr. Maria Faustina Kowalska. On September 28, 2008, he was declared Bl. Michael Sopocko at a special Mass at the Church of Divine Mercy in Bialystok. More than 80,000 faithful, including more than 100 bishops, archbishops, and the Cardinal Archbishops of Vilnius and Krakow, gathered on this fair September day with signs and colorful banners representing dioceses, parishes, and local church organizations. They came to celebrate the life of an extraordinary priest, the divinely chosen instrument for the spread of Divine Mercy throughout the world.

ABOUT THIS NEW EDITION OF
GOD IS MERCY

What would it have been like to listen to talks given by Bl. Michael Sopocko, and to learn about the mysteries of Divine Mercy directly from him? What would it have been like to have him as your spiritual director, and to be able to reflect on his words of guidance, challenge, and encouragement as he pointed out to you the path to ever greater holiness? Thousands of soldiers and seminarians had just that opportunity — and so did St. Faustina. My hope and prayer are that this book can enable us today to do so as well, if we meditate prayerfully on Bl. Sopocko's words, with a sincere desire to grow in the knowledge and love of our Merciful God.

The Congregation of Marian Fathers of the Immaculate Conception originally published this English translation of Bl. Sopocko's book *God is Mercy* in 1965. Of course, many things in the Roman Catholic Church, and in North American culture in particular, have changed since then, and this new edition reflects some of those changes. For example, most English-speaking Catholics no longer address God in prayer with the traditional forms "Thee" and "Thou," but instead more intimately as "You." The Divine Person we would often refer to as "the Holy Ghost," we now almost always call "the Holy Spirit." Gender specific language for human beings as well is no longer customary, so, for example, we rarely speak of "man" or "mankind" anymore, but use "humanity" or "humankind." Where it was not stylistically awkward to do so, therefore, I have tried to follow these new and common modes of expression.

No changes to the text were made merely to bow to the pressures of "political correctness," however; rather, the changes are solely for the sake of greater ease of comprehension by contemporary readers. For that reason, only the most archaic words and phrases from the original English edition of the text have been amended and replaced with current usage.

On occasion, I have also added a word or phrase that clarifies what Bl. Sopocko evidently was trying to convey (and where such an addition was most significant, I have indicated this to the reader by placing those words in brackets). However, no attempt has been made here to make a brand new translation of the text, or to "correct" the old one. My goal was to produce not so much a scholarly "critical edition" of this work, but a reasonably clear and accessible one, based on the good work already done in 1965.

More controversially, perhaps, I chose to retain the quotations from the Douay-Rheims version of the Bible that was used in the 1965 translation of this book. Although the Douay-Rheims translation of Holy Scripture is not widely used in English-speaking countries today, it is certainly closer to the translations of the Bible into Polish from the Latin Vulgate that Fr. Sopocko himself would have used, at least until the later years of his life. It seemed best to me, therefore, to accept the decision of the original translators, and continue to use that version of the Holy Scriptures in this new edition of Bl. Sopocko's work.

Also, I sincerely hope that the reader will find ample assistance in understanding Bl. Sopocko's rich and profound meditations in this volume by referring to the clarifications I have offered in the footnotes, as well as to my longer "Commentary" sections sprinkled throughout the text. As I have read and pondered his writings over the past few years, I have come to realize that in his role as a spiritual writer, Bl. Sopocko truly desires to make us *think*. His pastoral and spiritual guidance is never separated at any point from his training and wisdom as a theologian and teacher. That is a rare combination of gifts — and for that very reason, among many others, the works of Bl. Michael Sopocko are well worth reading today.

— **Dr. Robert Stackpole**
Director, John Paul II Institute of Divine Mercy

AUTHOR'S INTRODUCTION

"I have not concealed Thy Mercy and
Thy Truth from a great council"
— Psalm 39:11 [40:10][5]

The Mercy of God is a mystery that reason alone cannot entirely fathom. Indeed, reason shows us that God is Merciful, but on the other hand, it is unable to penetrate the depths into which Divine Mercy reaches. We draw knowledge of God's Mercy from the revelations given to us principally by Jesus Christ Himself. The psalmist speaks thus of Him: "I have not concealed Thy Mercy and Thy truth from a great council."

Our Savior did not conceal the Mercy of God, but revealed it through the Incarnation, through His hidden and public life. He emphasized it in His teachings, and above all, He presented it to us vividly through the mystery of the Redemption, by His death on the Cross for the sins of the whole world. All four of the Gospels, particularly that of St. Luke, teach us that God's Mercy is infinite.

The life of Jesus on earth was an inauguration of the Mercy that is to last and continue in the Church. Today it is no longer confined to Palestine, but is extended to the whole world; not only to the Galileans, but to all of humanity. All the graces of the Sacraments, sacramentals, indulgences, and charisms, and gifts and fruits of the Holy Spirit, are an unbroken torrent of Mercy flowing down on the faithful in His Church.

In the following chapters, we shall meditate on the Mercy of God. Let us do it with deep faith in the presence

---

[5] The Douay-Rheims translation here follows the enumeration of the Psalms in the Latin Vulgate version of the Bible. In contemporary English translations of the Old Testament, this passage can be found in Ps 40:10. Hereafter in this book, the enumeration of the Psalms in the RSVCE will be placed in brackets after each Psalm number from the Douay-Rheims version.

of the Most Merciful Father, Who sees us wherever we are; let us do it with special humility and contrition, in a spirit of penance for our sins; and moreover, with boundless trust in Him, Who said: "Take courage, I have overcome the world" (Jn 16:33).

Let us direct our meditation to practical ends as well, and above all, to the imitation and veneration of the Mercy of God. "Be merciful, therefore, even as your Father is Merciful" (Lk 6:36). Jesus commands us to be merciful, because on this depends our salvation: "Come, blessed of My Father ... as long as you did it for one of these, the least of my brethren, you did it for Me" (Mt 25:34 and 40). Therefore, after each meditation let us firmly resolve to perform some work of mercy to benefit the soul or the body of our neighbor, and these good works, in addition to prayer, will be the best means of glorifying the Mercy of God.

Finally, let us be like Christ: for "He did not conceal God's Mercy and truth from a great council," but made it known in His public and hidden life, in His teachings, in His Passion, and in His death. Therefore, we should not conceal the graces bestowed on us by God, but let us allow them to radiate and make them known to everyone, everywhere, so that we can say with the psalmist, "Let them that fear the Lord now say, that His Mercy endureth forever" (Ps 117 [116]:4).

— Bl. Michael Sopocko

Chapter 1

KNOWING GOD
IN THE MERCIFUL SAVIOR

"Now this is everlasting life, that they may
know Thee, the only true God, and Him,
Whom Thou hast sent, Jesus Christ"
— John 17:3

I. Human reason can have knowledge of God by observing the visible things of nature, but, on account of original sin, it attains truth only imperfectly and with great difficulty, especially the ultimate Truth — God. It was fitting, therefore, that God should become fully human in order to permit human beings to know Him more easily. *In the Person of Jesus Christ, God reveals Himself to the people.* In Him are seen all the perfections of God: "Philip, he who sees Me sees also the Father. How canst thou say, 'Show us the Father?' Dost thou not believe that I am in the Father and the Father in Me? The words that I speak to you I speak not on my own authority. But the Father dwelling in Me, it is He Who does the works. Do you believe that I am in the Father and the Father in Me? Otherwise believe because of the works themselves" (Jn 14:9-12). In this manner, in His teaching; through His whole life; and particularly by His Passion, death, Resurrection, and Ascension, Christ Our Lord gives us a clear message about God and His perfections.

People do not know God because they do not know Christ. "No one has at any time seen God. The only begotten Son, Who is in the bosom of the Father, He has revealed Him" (Jn 1:18).

Christ, a descendant of David through His blood relations, is a perfect Man. Yet He is also true God. Everything
that He brought and gave to humanity was longed for from
eternity and will have eternal worth. Let us not be misled
by His dress and manner of life, which followed the fashion
and customs of the Jews and Galileans, but rather let us pay
attention to what in Him has eternal meaning for us, and
what He bestowed on humankind: He revealed to us the
unfathomable perfections of God, and through this made
it possible for us to know and love God, and made us His
brothers and sisters, as well as adopted children of God.

*Jesus, I desire You, I look for You, I want to know You, for in
You will I know the Heavenly Father. Come, O Lord, and
enlighten me. I trust that Your Image will shine before me,
that Your Face will dispel the darkness in my soul, and
moreover that the radiance of Your Face will warm my
cold heart by enkindling in it the fire of Divine Love.*

II. "Now this is everlasting life, that they may know Thee" (Jn
17:3). Knowing God is life everlasting, or, plainly, it is Life. For
this reason, we often read that we possess eternal life already
on earth. "He who eats My flesh and drinks My blood has
life everlasting" (Jn 6:55). In his first Epistle, John the Apostle
says, "God has given us eternal life; and this life is in His Son.
He who has the Son has the life" (1 Jn 5:11-12). Elsewhere,
he states, "No murderer has eternal life abiding in him" (1 Jn
3:15); consequently, the just man has eternal life already in
this life.

What is "eternal life" in this life? It is sanctifying grace,
through which we become adopted children of God and
partakers of God's Life. On earth eternal life is concealed in
the darkness of worldliness, flesh, corruptibility, "[a]nd the
light shines in the darkness" (Jn 1:5), but its attributes will
be revealed in the future life. This future life will be not a
new one for the sons of the light, but rather a lifting of the

veil, when they stand before God, face to face. Therefore we possess eternal life already here on earth by knowing God in Christ, and through the grace of being God's adopted sons and daughters, and partakers of His Divine Life.

We attain a knowledge of God through our cooperation with Him. At Baptism, God pours into the soul the grace of faith, and it is the soul's part to cooperate with this grace. To the one who cooperates with God, He grants the gift of wisdom, which is so necessary in attaining higher perfection and sanctity, and a greater knowledge and love of God.[6] Thanks to this gift, the elect can walk in the presence of God and avoid sin. The gift of knowing God was bestowed on the apostles by the Holy Spirit at Pentecost. God does not usually grant this gift without our cooperation and preparation for it through fervent prayer, chastity and daily meditation.

I heartily want and desire to know You, O God! Therefore, I will guard the chastity of my thoughts, words, and deeds; I will meditate daily; and my prayer will be: "Kyrie eleison. Christe eleison." Lord, have mercy! Christ, have mercy!

O Jesus, grant me the spirit of wisdom, so that I may know God and have [the fullness of] eternal life.

---

[6] The Gift of Wisdom is granted to everyone at their Baptism, of course (see *Catechism*, 1266), and then strengthened (or increased) at their Confirmation (see *Catechism*, 1303). In other words, strictly speaking the Gift of Wisdom is not solely dependent upon us "cooperating with God." However, as Bl. Sopocko here implies, we need to cooperate with God by ridding ourselves of impediments to the operation of this gift (impediments such as inordinate attachments to worldly things — money, power, popularity, etc. — that obstruct God's work within us) and by following the impulses of the Holy Spirit in our hearts with docility. When we do this, then the gift of Wisdom within us can be put to use and operate more freely.

Chapter 2

GOD IS MERCY

"Your Father is Merciful"
— Luke 6:36

I. Who is God? "God is Love," says Holy Scripture (1 Jn 4:8), but this Love, directed toward human misery, is Mercy. That is why Christ Our Lord emphasizes this attribute of God: "Your Father is Merciful" (Lk 6:36).

We call a person merciful when he shows compassion for his neighbor and does all he can to lighten his neighbor's burdens whether material or spiritual. Mercy, as compassion, is even manifested in animals. For instance, a dog will whimper at the sight of its sick master. In the human soul, mercy enters not only as compassion (*passio*), but also as a moral virtue resulting from love of one's neighbor. The merciful Samaritan assisted the wounded Jew, and Cornelius, a pagan, showed mercy to the Israelites.

God's Mercy is neither compassion nor virtue. He, as the purest Spirit, is not subject to any affection,[7] nor is His Mercy

---

[7] This is the opinion of the Thomistic heritage of philosophy and theology, which Fr. Sopocko often followed, but it has not been defined (at least, not without qualification) as the official teaching of the Catholic Church. For example, Pope St. John Paul II in *Dominum et Vivificantem*, no. 39, taught that our human capacity for affection and sympathetic compassion hint at something analogous — and even more perfect — in God:

> The concept of God as the necessarily most perfect being excludes from God any pain deriving from deficiencies or wounds; but in the depths of God there is a Father's love that, faced with man's sin, in the language of the Bible reacts so deeply as to say "I am sorry that I have made him" ... The Sacred Book speaks to us of a Father who feels compassion for man, as though sharing his pain. In the end, this inscrutable and indescribable fatherly "pain" will bring about above all the wonderful economy of redemptive love in Jesus Christ ... in whose humanity the "suffering" of God is concretized.

a virtue, because into human mercy enters a certain sadness in which He has no part, since He is essentially self-sufficient and perfectly happy. Divine Mercy is God's perfection or attribute in which He willingly inclines Himself toward His creatures to ward off impending miseries and to satisfy their daily needs.

God, as the most perfect Being, is Spirit most pure and most simple; that is, He is not composed of separate elements. He is a oneness with no components in His nature. It is true that in God there are three Persons Who are distinct, one from the other, by procession, but in His nature God is one, indivisible, eternal. "One there is Who is good, and He is God" (Mt 19:17).

Human reason is incapable of expressing the whole perfection of God in one concept and consequently it raises all the perfections in creatures to the highest degree and attributes them to God. Hence, we speak of God's Wisdom, Patience, Justice, Providence, etc. Furthermore, for a better knowledge of God we reduce His perfections to two groups. In the first, we refer them to His nature (for instance: Infinity, Immutability, Eternity), and we call them absolute perfections, and in the other, we refer them to His relation with His creatures and call them relative perfections. The latter are manifested in God's works and are noticed more easily. By meditating on the depths of these relative attributes we acquire a better understanding of God. For this reason, the fathers of the First Vatican Council (1870) pointed out that God is known best by being studied through His creatures. In other words, they encouraged us to study His relative perfections and to compare the one with the other. Goodness, Generosity, Providence, and Justice are the relative attributes of God most frequently mentioned in the Scriptures, but most of all His Mercy is praised. The Mercy of God is therefore a relative perfection or attribute, through which, in Holy Scripture, God most commonly expresses His relation to His creatures and through which we can comprehend our Creator, Redeemer and Sanctifier. This attribute, as well as the others, does not differ substantially from the essence of God.[8] In other words, God's Mercy is God Himself pitying our misery and satisfying our needs.

Holy Scripture praises the Mercy of God separately from His other attributes, but this is mere condescension permitting the human mind, despite its weakness, to understand to a certain extent the nature of God. The human mind usually grasps a whole by analyzing its parts. If separate parts do not exist in a being, as in the case of God, the human mind proceeds through analogy and substitutes for them some corresponding elements that it finds in other things.

II. The Mercy of God is inferred from the very notion of God, Who is Himself the First Act, the First Perfection, the First Good, independent of every other. Human beings acquire the virtue of mercy like any other virtue, from God, just as the moon reflects rays from the sun.

The Mercy of God, which does not depend on anything, is unlimited and infinite. On the contrary, human mercy depends on the love of one's neighbor and of God, Who fixes its mode, measures, and limits. God manifests His Mercy without using any intermediate form. Human mercy flows from love of one's neighbor, which love, in turn, rises and grows dependent on acts and forms proper to it.

God is always perfectly merciful, for He is immutable [that is, unchangeable]; but human mercy can grow, lessen, or even disappear, as in great sinners.

> *I trust in You, O God, Whom I cannot think of as being less than the most Merciful Father, regarding me with pity, ever desirous of raising me from my wretchedness and ever eager to supply all my wants.*

---

[8] What Bl. Sopocko means here is that, since God is Spirit, and does not have "parts" (as bodily creatures do), then whatever is attributed to God simply is God Himself, His perfect Being in eternal act, seen from a particular angle. Thus, according to this classical Catholic view, Divine Mercy is not a part or distinct aspect of God, but simply another name for God's "essence," that is, what God essentially and always is.

Chapter 3

LET US TRUST IN GOD

"Take courage; it is I, do not be afraid"
— Mark 6:50

I. Christ is calling the apostles to trust in Him when they are in danger at the time of the storm on the sea. The psalmist, finding himself in great danger, places his trust firmly in the Merciful God. "But I have trusted in Thy Mercy. My heart shall rejoice in Thy salvation" (Ps 12:6 [13:5]). When we find ourselves exposed to dangers, in regard to either soul or body, we should trust in God, lest we fall. The basis of this trust is the fathomless Mercy of God, His Omnipotence, and His infinite Wisdom.

To trust is to expect help, either promised or understood. This is not a separate [human] virtue,[9] but an indispensable condition of the virtue of hope, and at the same time part of the virtues of fortitude and magnanimity. Being a component of both the latter virtues, it unites them and in so doing gives us the foundation for a truly strong character.

Trust is a great lever in our life, even if we expect only human help. But many events in history have proved that human help is deceptive, promises are uncertain, and alliances often treacherous. On the contrary, our trust in God is never liable to deception. "But Mercy shall encompass him that hopeth in the Lord" (Ps 31 [32]:10), says the psalmist on the basis of revelation and personal experience, emphasizing God's Mercy as the chief foundation of trust.

The poor shepherd David goes forth to battle against

---

[9] By "virtue" Bl. Sopocko means a firm attitude and stable disposition of the soul to do what is right and good. See *Catechism of the Catholic Church*, 1804, and 1833-1834.

the well-equipped Philistine giant, whom he defeats because
he trusted in God's help. "Thou comest to me with a sword,
and with a spear, and with a shield: but I come to thee in the
name of the Lord of hosts" (1 Sam 17:45). This same David
reproaches himself in other instances for excessive fear, and
for a lack of trust in God. "Why art thou sad, O my soul?
And why dost thou trouble me? Hope in God" (Ps 41 [42]:6).
"Therefore we will not fear when the earth shall be troubled;
and the mountains shall be removed into the heart of the sea"
(Ps 45 [46]:2). "And I will go in to the altar of God: to God
Who giveth joy to my youth" (Ps 42 [43]:4). Indeed, youth is
a period of trust. But the soul does not age in its relation to
God; it is ever rejuvenated according to the measure of its
growth in trust.

II. The Old Testament was only the pattern and figure of the
New Law. How much more, then, should we reproach ourselves for our lack of trust in the Savior, than did the psalmist
of old! Through the most tender words and pictures does Jesus
call to the soul to follow Him with a childlike simplicity and
trust. "I am," He says, "the good Shepherd" (Jn 10:11), and it is
this title that should awaken boundless trust in every heart. In
relation to the Heavenly Father, our Lord Jesus places Himself
like a Lamb, laid out as a holocaust for the sins of the world;
and in relation to us, He likens Himself to a Good Shepherd,
Who knows and loves His flock, feeding us with grace, with
doctrine, and with His most Holy Body and Blood.

On other occasions, Christ speaks of Himself in familiar
images and intimate expressions. He is to us as a hen that
gathers her chickens under her wings. The sight of our delib-
erate sins, and of the unfaithfulness of sinners, brings tears
to His eyes and the saddest of complaints from His Merciful
Heart: "Jerusalem, Jerusalem! Thou who killest the prophets
and stonest those who are sent to thee!" (Mt 23:37).

Why does the Savior place such moving scenes before
our eyes, if not to awaken our trust? How could Jesus, so
Merciful to Jerusalem, so tender to the prodigal son, to the

public sinner Magdalen, to Peter, and to the thief on the cross, be severe to those who believe in Him and strive to keep His commandments? Throughout His life Christ exhibited the greatest Mercy, and His attitude toward us has not decreased in even the smallest degree today. Could God, in His boundless Wisdom, find anything more appropriate to encourage us to intimacy with Himself and to limitless trust? Would our Redeemer so indefatigably encourage us to trust in Him, if He did not want to reward this trust with Mercy? Most certainly He is infallible and does not want to lead us into error.

Jesus, I trust in You. I trust that You will forgive my sins, and that You have prepared Heaven for me. I trust that You will provide all the graces I need to save my soul.

Chapter 4

LET US LOVE GOD

"I am the Lord, thy God ...
showing Mercy unto many thousands,
to them that love Me,
and keep My commandments"
— Deuteronomy 5:6, 10

I. Our love for God is one of the chief motives that prompt Him to bestow His Mercy on us. While our trust leads us to the foot of the mountain of God's Mercy, love discovers its peak and brings back from it tokens of infinite Mercy for our souls. Our love of God is a heavenly fire that shapes our every virtue, imparting to it a value with which eternal life is merited. Love is the first and greatest commandment, in which all others are contained. We are created to love God, and for this reason alone He endowed us with intellect and will. Love of God, then, is our start, our means, and our final end. Does a father expect his children to be hard-hearted? Does God not require from us, His intelligent creatures, a tender tribute of love? Love is not only the essence, but also the summary of our perfection, and the queen of all virtues: "Love God," says St. Augustine, "and do whatever you will."[10]

---

[10] In quoting St. Augustine, Bl. Sopocko presumes the Christian definition of "love" in doing "whatever you will." Today, "love" all too often is reduced to sentimental, emotional experiences, but as Pope Benedict XVI reminds us in his encyclical *Deus Caritas Est* (2005), authentic love is revealed in Christ's crucifixion. When we love as Christ has loved — even unto death — then we can "do whatever we will," because our love always will be guided by, and a reflection of His own, and when our will is guided by His love, then it will always be ordered according to the law of God as revealed in the teachings of His Church.

The object of love is that good in which we find delight. The object of the theological virtue[11] of love is God as the greatest Good. Goodness is the infinite perfection of His nature, embracing any existing perfection in the highest degree. God, as Goodness, may be considered either as good for us, the One from Whose Mercy we receive gifts and graces; or as Good in Himself, worthy of the highest love and delight, regardless of whether we consider Him to be such or not. In the former case this love is desire and in the latter it is benevolence.

In the latter case, we love God, not because He shows Mercy toward us, but because He Himself *is* Goodness, Truth, and Beauty. Such love is perfect love. On the other hand, loving God on account of His benefits, though it is a foundation for the theological virtue of hope, is imperfect love. However, this imperfect love, which arises from meditating on and understanding the benefits of the infinite Mercy of God, tends toward perfect love, which is love of God purely and simply because He is Good.

II. What is to be understood by this Divine Goodness, which is lovable in Itself? Some theologians think that the nature of God, including all His attributes, is natural Divine Goodness. There is, however, a more common opinion that *every* divine attribute, even known separately, is natural Divine Goodness. Every attribute, therefore, can be an object of perfect love. So, for instance, the Mercy of God as such is worthy of being loved because this Mercy really contains in Itself the divine nature including all Its attributes. Moreover, if we love the Mercy of God explicitly in Itself, we implicitly love the whole divine nature with all its attributes.

In our wayfaring state we experience the Mercy of God more than any other divine attribute, and we recognize it more easily. Thus through our devotion to Divine Mercy we easily

---

[11] In the Catholic Tradition the "theological virtues" are those virtues infused into our soul by the Holy Spirit that lead us most directly to God: faith, hope, and love (see 1 Cor 13: 13).

arouse in our hearts a love of God: a love at first imperfect, later becoming a perfect love having for its object the Mercy of God Itself, aside from all personal benefit. For instance, God's Goodness arouses in us adoration; His Justice, fear; His Wisdom, admiration. But His Mercy, by which we know Him as a compassionate Father, arouses in us confidence, a foundation of love as desire; and then a perfect love as benevolence and gratitude. If meditation on the works of the Mercy of God be added to this love, it is difficult to imagine anything of divine origin more capable of leading souls to perfection.

Our love of God is a result of cooperating with God's graces. God infuses in our souls the grace of love at Baptism; but it is up to us to cooperate with this grace. To make baptismal grace grow in our souls, we must awaken acts of love of God, bear sufferings and contradictions in a spirit of love, and above all avoid sin and beg the Holy Spirit for the gift of Love and Wisdom. The Holy Spirit is an utterance of Love from the Father to the Son and from the Son to the Father, and therefore He is called Love.

"Come Holy Spirit, fill the hearts of Your faithful and enkindle in them the fire of Your Love."

Chapter 5

I BELIEVE IN GOD

"For he who comes to God
must believe that God exists"
— Hebrews 11:6

I. The root of love, and the fountain of trust, is faith. "Now, faith is the substance of things to be hoped for, the evidence of things that are not seen" (Heb 11:1). In order to expect God's help, or rather to trust in His Mercy, it is necessary, first of all, to believe that God exists; that He has promised to help us; that He will not refuse to help us, since He is Merciful; and that He can always help us, since He is Almighty. To love God, it is necessary, above all, to believe that He Himself is infinitely perfect and worthy of our love, that everything we have and all that we are we owe to His infinite Mercy.

Faith can be an act and a virtue. An act of faith is to acknowledge as true that which God has revealed. We can most certainly recognize the fact of revelation, since in a revelation God usually gives His signature and His seal of truth; the signature is His miracles, and the seal of truth is His prophecies. Although the words and actions of Christ show Divine Wisdom and Power, He principally stresses His miracles, the greatest of all being the Resurrection. This is the signature and seal of truth that Christ was sent by the Father: "these very works that I do, bear witness to me, that the Father has sent me" (Jn 5:36). God cannot err, nor does He lead others into error. Consequently, we should accept with faith everything that Christ taught.

Certain revealed truths are inaccessible to reason (mysteries) or arouse difficulties on the part of reason. Reason alone cannot assent to a given truth of the supernatural order, since it has as its object natural truths only; therefore, the influence of the will is needed so that reason may recognize as true that which it does not naturally comprehend. However, the will is not able to exert this influence without grace. Hence, in the very act of faith the grace of God is required to exert its influence on reason, through enlightenment as to a given truth. And grace must likewise exert its influence on the will, so that it may strongly desire to believe and may encourage reason to submit to the truths of faith. "To believe is an act of reason professing the Divine Truth, at the command of the will, moved by God's grace" (Council of Trent, session 2, a.9). So it is through the Mercy of God that we can make an act of faith.

II. As a virtue, faith inseparably follows sanctifying grace and is as necessary for salvation as grace itself. God infuses faith into the soul at Baptism and for this reason it is called an infused virtue. We lose it only through sins against faith (apostasy, infidelity). Other mortal sins do not completely remove the virtue of faith, but only deform it through the lack of love of God. Hence, it is evident that also in the virtue of faith, God's Mercy is preeminent above all else.

In faith, then, the Chief Author is God, both in the act and in the virtue. The grace of the infinite Mercy of God calls us to faith, develops it, and sustains it even in a sinner. Therefore, we should, for our part, actively cooperate through the humble acquiescence of our reason and the surrender to Divine Authority.

God could have created human beings full of wisdom, so that we would understand all the truths that we now know only from revelation. But such a creature would have no greatness, no true freedom, nor any possibility of attaining perfection and merits. "He who does not believe shall be condemned" (Mk 16:16). Why did Christ oblige us to believe? In order to give us the opportunity to gain virtues and merits and at the same time to increase and be perfected in our love of God.

Faith and the deeds resulting from it are so inseparable that without these deeds, faith slowly disappears. A person at first shortens his prayers, then slowly neglects them, does not frequent the Sacraments, does not observe fast or abstinence, does not perform acts of mercy toward his neighbor, hears Holy Mass without recollection, and eventually completely omits Mass and falls into spiritual lethargy.[12] His zeal diminishes, distaste for and aversion to things of God are born in his heart, and finally there comes unbelief. "O thou of little faith, why didst thou doubt?" (Mt 14:31), the Savior rebukes Peter for lack of faith, pointing out that the observance and growth of faith depend on us. If this were not so, Jesus' reprimand would have been unfounded.

I resolve to be zealous in observing practices and deeds that faith dictates to me. I will make frequent acts of faith in all revealed truths.
"I do believe, Lord. Help my unbelief" (Mk 9:24).

---

[12] By "hearing" Mass, Bl. Sopocko is referring to the time, prior to the liturgical reforms initiated by Vatican II, when the manner of lay participation in the Mass was different. It tended to focus primarily upon hearing and listening to the priest in the Liturgy (sometimes while saying private devotional prayers during the offering of the Eucharistic Prayer in Latin by the priest), and often not did not include reception of Holy Communion.

Chapter 6

MERCY OF GOD, SUPREME ATTRIBUTE OF THE CREATOR

"The mercies of God are above all His works"
— Psalm 144 [145]:9

I. Glorifying the Mercy of God with a deluge of words, the inspired psalmist does not hesitate to place it above all His other attributes: that is, he considers God's Mercy His greatest relative perfection.

God's relationship to His creatures manifests itself in removing their deficiencies and in providing them with perfections. This act of provision, when it is considered independently of any circumstances, is attributed to the Goodness of God. God's complete disinterestedness[13] in distributing benefits to us is ascribed to His Generosity. Providence is divine solicitude that we may attain our final end by cooperating with God's grace. God's bestowal of perfections according to a prearranged plan and order is called the Justice of God.[14] Finally, God's providing His creatures with perfections in order to supply their needs and lead them

---

[13] By "disinterestedness," Bl. Sopocko does not mean that God is indifferent to us. Rather, he means that, because God is infinitely perfect and needs nothing for Himself, there is no self-interest involved in His relationship with His creatures; all that God does is for our good above all.

[14] Notice that, quite often for Fr. Sopocko, Divine "Justice" does not have the same meaning that we normally give to the word in English. It is not merely the attribute by which God renders to each and everyone what is their due, for all the good or evil they have done. It includes such penal justice, but goes well beyond it. Blessed Sopocko, following the classical Catholic Tradition, often uses the word "Justice" to refer to the divine attribute by which God seeks to bring to proper order His whole creation, setting all things right according to His wise and loving plan.

out of their miseries is called the Mercy of God. Therefore, we distinguish five chief attributes of God in His relations with creatures: Goodness, Generosity, Providence, Justice, and Mercy. To these we subordinate all secondary operative attributes of God (e.g., Patience is subordinate to Mercy).

If we consider the works of God from different points of view, we can discover these perfections in all of them. The preservation of Moses, who was placed in a basket on the river Nile, if considered generally and independently of any circumstances, is attributed to the Goodness of God. If, however, we consider that this preservation was neither necessary for God nor merited by the infant, we may conclude that God acted disinterestedly, that is, He acted out of Generosity. Furthermore, we attribute God's watchfulness over the infant floating on the river to His Providence. But this preservation of Moses, in accordance with the divine plan of leading the Israelites out of Egypt, is called the Justice of God. Finally, God's raising of Moses out of the hardships that endangered him on every side, and providing him with perfections such as the necessities of life, growth, and education, is the work of His Mercy.

Of all the distressing moments in the life of the child Moses, the one that strikes us most is the misery of his being abandoned on such a large river, and the needs that would soon arise therefrom. Therefore, we may rightly say that the Goodness of God is nothing else but Mercy that creates and endows; Generosity is Mercy that is unusually liberal with gifts; Providence is Mercy that is constantly vigilant; Justice is Mercy that rewards over and above merits, and punishes far less than is deserved; finally, Love of God is Mercy that has compassion on our wretchedness and draws us to Itself. Hence, when we reflect in our human way, the Mercy of God seems to be the chief motive for His exterior actions and, as St. Thomas asserts, is found at the very source of every work of the Creator.

II. The Angelic Doctor proves this truth in the following argument. Every perfection may be considered either in itself or in regard to the one in whom it is found. Mercy considered in itself is the highest perfection because it consists in communicating one's own perfections to other beings by lifting them from their wretchedness and removing their deficiencies; one who gives shows higher perfection than the one who receives. Such communicativeness is a property of higher beings in regard to the lower; in the highest degree, it is a property of God through which His Greatest Power is manifested.

Considered in a person in whom it is found, mercy is not always the highest perfection, but is so only if the possessor himself is the highest being; that is, if he has neither an equal nor anyone superior to himself. The one, therefore, who has some superior to himself manifests his perfection best by partaking in a higher being through love, more than by removing deficiencies in lower beings. For this reason, love of God is the greatest [human] virtue. Since God has no superior and no one to whom He could subordinate Himself through love, therefore His highest perfection is not Love, but Mercy (*Summa Theologiae*, I, q.21, aa. 3 and 4; II-II, q. 30, a.4). Furthermore, comparing Mercy with Justice, the Angelic Doctor proves that Mercy is superior. This is also confirmed by Holy Scripture, which directly states: "but mercy triumphs over judgment" (Jas 2:13).

In moments of trial, I will recall with joy the infinite Mercy of God and humbly submit myself to the Divine Will, trusting that in the end everything will change to good in the hand of Him, Whose "ways are Mercy and Truth" (Ps 24 [25]:10).

Chapter 7

MERCY OF GOD, GREATEST PERFECTION OF THE REDEEMER

"Men and beasts Thou wilt preserve, O Lord:
O how hast Thou multiplied Thy Mercy, O God!"
— Psalm 35:7-8 [36:6-7]

I. In the eyes of God everything is miserable and full of imperfections. Yet the greatest misery is sin. God would not be God if He let sin prevail without just punishment, since "He wills His glory to no one" and will not permit Himself to be mocked. For this reason, a horrible, eternal punishment immediately befell the rebellious angels. The same could happen to us when we sin. However, the Son of God resolved to become our Redeemer, to give Himself as a perfect sacrifice of compensation to the Heavenly Father for human sin. "Then said I, Behold I come" (Ps 39:8 [40:7]).

The greatest evidence of God's Mercy is that His Son found a means unheard of, unique, unfailing, inconceivable, worthy of admiration and ecstatic praise. He resolved to take our human nature, so that in it and through it He might reform human nature and bring salvation to all of humanity. Only He, since He was equal to God the Father and at the same time a man, could give God's Majesty worthy satisfaction for the offense of original and actual sin, and establish a treasury, from which in the future it would be possible to draw continually in reparation for sin. If He were not God, He would be unable to obtain adequately the pardon humanity was in need of, and appease the offended Majesty of God. If, however, He were not human, He could not have given us a fitting example of how to seek forgiveness, nor would He have made worthy satisfaction in the name of all of humankind.[15]

---

[15] When Bl. Sopocko writes of Christ on the Cross making "satisfaction" for our sins and "appeasing" the divine "wrath" or the "offended Divine Majesty," he was using traditional theological language that has largely gone out of fashion, since it can be so easily misunderstood by people today: as if God has a petulant and vindictive side to His nature that must be "bought off" by the sufferings and death of Jesus before He is willing to forgive us! That is not, of course, what Bl. Sopocko or the Catholic Tradition meant to say. Rather, the biblical language about divine "wrath" and the traditional notion of God's "offended Divine Majesty" are metaphors for Divine Justice, which is the attribute by which God orders all things rightly according to His eternal plan for creation, and with regard to human sin in particular, the attribute by which He ultimately renders to each and all precisely what is their due for all the good and evil they have done (e.g. Mt 16:27; Rom 2:6-8; 2 Cor 5:10; Rev 2:23).

If we all received precisely what was due to us for our sins on the scales of Divine Justice, however, our situation would be hopeless! Through the unity of all the divine attributes in the nature of God, Divine Justice can never be separated from His Love and His Mercy. (On the unity of all the divine attributes, for example, see what Bl. Sopocko wrote in Chapter 2, above.) God is always perfectly merciful and perfectly just in all that He does. Indeed, St. Thomas Aquinas taught that "the work of divine justice always presupposes the work of mercy and is based on it" (*Summa Theologiae*, I, 21, 4) — in other words, when God responds to fallen humanity with His justice, it is never merely an act of vindictiveness on His part; it always in some way furthers His purposes of mercy as well (see, for example, Heb 12:6).

On Calvary, God permitted sinful humanity to put His beloved Son to death on a Cross. In this way, out of His great love for us, through His divine Son, He fashioned the work of our redemption out of humanity's greatest moral crime. God through Christ accomplished for us what we could never do for ourselves (see 2 Cor 5:19), that is, the atoning sacrifice (or "satisfaction" of divine justice) for our sins (see Is 53:5-6): "But he was wounded for our transgressions, he was bruised for our iniquities; upon him was the chastisement that made us whole, and with his stripes we are healed." In short, on the Cross the Son of God fulfilled the need for justice and mercy in response to human sin at one and the same time. That is why St. Paul can sum it all up by writing in his epistle to the Romans: "God shows his love for us in that while we were yet sinners, Christ died for us" (Rom 5:8). In his encyclical *Dives in Misericordia* (1981), Pope St. John Paul II expressed in contemporary theological language what Bl. Sopocko doubtless intended to convey about the unity of Divine Justice and Divine Mercy manifest on the Cross:

> In the Passion and Death of Christ — in the fact that the Father did not spare His own Son, but "for our sake made him sin" — absolute justice is expressed, for Christ undergoes the passion and cross because of the sins of humanity. This constitutes even a "superabundance" of justice, for the sins of man are "compensated for" by the sacrifice of the Man-God. Nevertheless, this justice, which is properly justice "to God's measure," springs completely from love: from the love of the Father and the Son, and completely bears fruit in love. ... The divine dimension of the redemption is put into effect not only by bringing justice to bear on sin, but also by restoring to love that creative power in man, thanks to

"Lord, Thou hast blessed Thy land: Thou hast turned away the captivity of Jacob. Thou hast forgiven the iniquity of Thy people: thou hast covered all their sins" (Ps 84:2-3 [85:1-2]), exclaims the psalmist in joyous rapture, while prophesying the release of the human race from the bondage of Satan and humanity's rising from the state of sin to the state of grace. He might well say, Thou hast covered all the sins of humanity with the wounds of Thy Son, Thou hast appeased Thy just anger against us, Thou hast restrained Thyself in the severity of Thy zeal for justice, while accepting the intercession of Thine only begotten Son. Therefore, Thou wilt not be angered at Thy creatures, but Thou wilt extend Thy Mercy, "for generation upon generation" (Lk 1:50).

II. "Blessed be the God and the Father of Our Lord Jesus Christ, Who according to His great Mercy has begotten us again ... unto a living hope" (1 Pet 1:3), says the Apostle Peter, stressing the infinite Mercy of God in Redemption. Similarly, the Church in its Liturgy praises the merciful might of the Redemption, as, for instance, on Holy Saturday in the prayer after the ninth prophecy: "to have made the world in the beginning was no more excellent work than to have immolated Christ, our paschal Victim ... in the end of the ages."[16] In the collect for the tenth Sunday after Pentecost the Spouse of Christ [that is, the Church] plainly speaks of the Mercy of God showed to us in the Redemption. Who, while meditating on the above truths, will not be astonished? Who can refrain from tears of gratitude, when reflecting on the words that our Savior spoke to Nicodemus, "For God so loved the world that He gave His only begotten Son, that those who believe in Him

---

which he once more has access to the fullness of life and holiness that comes from God. In this way, redemption involves the revelation of mercy in its fullness. (no. 7)

[16] A similar prayer in the revised Roman Missal today would be this one from the prayer after the first reading in the current Easter Vigil liturgy:

God, who wonderfully created human nature
and still more wonderfully redeemed it, grant us, we pray,
to set our minds against the enticements of sin,
that we may merit to attain eternal joys.

may not perish, but may have life everlasting" (Jn 3:16). In other words, God has so greatly and deeply pitied the misery of man, the lowest, most ungrateful rational creature, who has deserved eternal punishment, that He has given, not an angel, a cherub or seraph, but His only begotten Son as Lord, Teacher, and Priest; as an example; and as the price and Sacrifice of the Passion and Crucifixion that could satisfy His Majesty. The divine nature of the Son was united with human nature in order to save human beings and raise them to the dignity of adopted filiation with God.

As all lower creatures on earth were placed at humanity's disposal, so through our Redemption and elevation to the dignity of God's children, all these creatures have been included in the plan of Providence. Even inanimate objects, houses, dwellings, food, and clothing, are instruments, which, while serving humanity, serve God also. "Men and beasts Thou wilt preserve, O Lord: O how hast Thou multiplied Thy Mercy, O God!" (Ps 35:7-8 [36:6-7]).

In the Redemption God has enabled us through Christ to share in His holiness. God is Holy in His very being; we become holy through the graces of Mercy. The holiness of God is infinite and cannot change; we, however, can increase or decrease in holiness or even lose it completely.

I will base my sanctification on my Redeemer, Who "alone is Holy, alone is the Lord, alone is the Most High" (Gloria in excelsis).

Chapter 8

MERCY OF GOD, UNFATHOMABLE LOVE OF THE SANCTIFIER

"The charity of God is poured forth in our hearts by the Holy Spirit"
— Romans 5:5

I. The mutual love of God the Father and God the Son finds expression in the third Person of the Trinity, the Holy Spirit, Who is called Love because He is the common breath of their love. He is also called Holy because in His essence He is particularly related to holiness. Holiness depends above all on the simplicity and purity of the will and of love. The Holy Spirit is nothing else but all purity, simplicity, goodness, and love which are immense, unchanging, powerful and sublime.

The Holy Spirit is holiness not only because He is expression of the holiness of God, the very essence of holiness, but also because He distributes holiness to creatures, being therefore a gift of God; a pledge; a prototype, source, and author of all graces of God. Through Him man is born into Divine life with the water of Baptism (Jn 3:5). He justifies humanity through penance (Jn 20:23). He pours supernatural virtues into our hearts. He is the author of the grace which absolves us from sin and endows us with purity and holiness; but above all He is the bond of charity (Rom 5:5) between humanity and God.

II. The love of the Holy Spirit, the Sanctifier, with regard to creatures is, in reality, Mercy. We distinguish between natural, sensual love and intellectual, spiritual love; the latter may be love [springing from] desire (concupiscence),[17] if we seek benefits from the person loved, or it may be love [flowing from] benevolence, if we solely wish good to the person loved. One kind of love of benevolence is friendship, which exists between persons more or less equal, who know each other and wish each other good.

God's love toward humanity cannot consist in love of desire, because He neither receives nor derives any benefit from it.[18] We cannot call this love friendship either, for the indispensable condition — equality — is lacking. True, Christ calls the apostles His friends (Jn 15:14), but He says this only as the God-Man to men, whom He raised through His Mercy to participation in Divine Life. Hence there remains the simple love of benevolence, which differs according to whether it is bestowed on superiors or equals, or on inferiors.

The motive of the love of benevolence in relation to equal or superior beings is an absolute good, or rather a recognition of and delight in the absolute perfections of the beloved person. As for God, He cannot see in any creatures absolute perfections, since He alone possesses such perfection. Neither does He notice in them apparent "absolute" perfections,

---

[17] In Catholic theology, "concupiscence" commonly refers to disordered desires within us that incline us to sin (see *Catechism*, 1264 and 1426). Blessed Sopocko, however, seems to be using the word here in the more nuanced way of the Thomistic school of theology: Love springing from "concupiscence" ("concupiscible love") signifies an imperfect form of love in which someone loves a thing, not that he might wish the good in itself *to* that thing, but rather that he might wish to appropriate that good *for himself.* By loving in this way, we seek for ourselves some authentic good, including those things that are useful or delightful to us. For example, one might love one's family because family life can provide us with the comfort, support, and companionship we need. By contrast, love flowing from "benevolence" in the Thomistic tradition refers to disinterested affection, selfless seeking of the good of another (akin to the New Testament word *agape)*; for example, one might selflessly love one's family, seeking to meet its legitimate needs even at the cost of great sacrifice to oneself.

[18] Blessed Sopocko does not mean by this that God does not desire our good, but when we use the word "desire" in this way of God, we need to recognize that it is not the same as human desire, because it does not come from any "need" on God's part (since He is infinitely perfect, and therefore needs nothing). We may think of it, paradoxically, as a selfless desire for our good, with no need or self-seeking in it at all.

which creatures sometimes notice in each other, since He recognizes everything most perfectly.

The motive of love of benevolence of superior beings toward lower beings is a relative good or rather a recognition of and delight in such perfections that are not devoid of some defects and are exposed to various misfortunes. For example, a man may take a liking to a horse, not only because it is useful, but also because he delights in its stature, speed, and other valuable characteristics that the horse can lose, unless they are carefully preserved by the master. Generally, such love is mercy, for it tends to lift an inferior object from its misery by keeping it from various defects.

With such love God loves His rational creatures, especially human beings, because He sees in us a relative good that He Himself imparted. Moreover, since He continuously preserves and develops this good, by perpetually interceding, watching over us, removing our deficiencies, and lifting us up from various miseries, we can safely say that He constantly displays His Mercy. Therefore, this love of God toward His rational creatures is Mercy. Such Mercy or Love is the highest perfection of God in His relation to the world. So, together with St. Thomas Aquinas, we may ascertain with equal right that God's Mercy as well as His Love — which is Mercy in relation to human beings — is His highest relative attribute. Hence all expressions in the Holy Scriptures that indicate God's Love for us can be replaced with one word, Mercy. "God so loved the world" — God so pitied the world and showed Mercy (Jn 3:16). "According to His Mercy He saved us, through the bath of regeneration and renewal by the Holy Spirit" (Tit 3:5).

With childlike trust I will turn to the Holy Spirit as to the source of the unfathomable Love or Mercy of the Sanctifier; I will invoke His aid in all my concerns, even external ones, imploring Him to supply what is lacking in my reason, prudence and other abilities, and praying to Him from the bottom of my heart: "Come Holy Spirit, Spirit of Love, Spirit of Mercy."

COMMENTARY:
THE MERCIFUL TRIUNE GOD
LOVES US INTO BEING

Where does Divine Mercy come from? This sounds like an easy question at first. After all, if it is Divine Mercy, surely it must come from God, because He alone is "divine."

True enough, but if we asked that question of Bl. Michael Sopocko, as an experienced theology professor and spiritual director, he would say that the matter is not so simple; we need to go deeper. There is a richness to the nature of God that many Catholics do not appreciate. We tend to forget that God is not a divine person, but three Divine Persons, and it is from the mystery of the eternal love between the Father, the Son, and the Holy Spirit that the merciful love of God for His creatures always flows. Saint Faustina herself once prayed: "Divine Mercy, fountain gushing forth from the mystery of the Most Blessed Trinity, I trust in You" (*Diary*, 949). Blessed Sopocko put it this way:

> No one is able to comprehend the tenderness, the glowing love, and the supreme happiness with which the Father, from eternity, is always generating the Son, and the Holy Spirit proceeding from the Son and the Father. All the brilliance, fire, and joy of the love that acts, enlivens, and inflames creatures is only a very weak reflection of the eternal generation of the Son by the Father and of the surge and procession of the Holy Spirit from the blazing Ocean of Divine Love that exists between the Father and the Son (*God is Mercy*, chapter 9).

In fact, as Bl. Sopocko teaches us, this awesome, eternal love among the persons of the Blessed Trinity is infinitely perfect, so that God had absolutely no need to create anything

50

else at all. He was perfectly happy and blessed in Himself. So why did He bother to do it? The truth must be, Bl. Sopocko states (and in this he follows closely the teachings of St. Thomas Aquinas), that God chose to create a world out of merciful love for creatures themselves: to bestow on them a finite share in His infinite perfections, and above all to enable them to experience the perfect love that is eternally shared among the Persons of the Trinity.

God's "natural goodness" is manifest in the mutual love of the Persons of the Blessed Trinity, Bl. Sopocko tells us, and that is more than enough to account for His eternal happiness. Since He needs nothing at all for Himself, His decision to create the world — ourselves included — can only be an expression of His "mercy": the kind of love that always seeks to meet the needs and relieve the miseries of others. As Bl. Sopocko puts it: "Divine Mercy is God's perfection or attribute in which He willingly inclines Himself toward His creatures to ward off impending miseries and to satisfy their daily needs" (chapter 2). In other words, God saw that the first and most urgent need of creatures was the need to be, to exist. So, out of His merciful, compassionate love, He offered them the chance to share in His eternal joy by creating them to be the objects of that love:

> Lack of existence, or nothingness, is the greatest of all wants and the most extreme misery. All nature shudders before such misery. Every animal, and every human being, flees from this want, fearing it above all other sufferings and wants, proving thus that lack of existence is the greatest of all miseries. So creation of the world with all its beings is the work of the Mercy of God, which may also be called Divine Goodness in relation to the supreme misery of nonexistence (*God is Mercy*, chapter 12).

Father Sopocko's spiritual "directee," St. Faustina, understood this mystery as well. She writes about it in her *Diary*, entries 1741 and 423:

> O God, who [is] happiness in Your very self, and [has]
> no need of creatures to make You happy, because
> Yourself You are the fullness of love, yet out of Your
> fathomless mercy You call creatures into being, and
> grant them a share in Your eternal happiness and
> in Your life, that divine and indwelling life in which
> You live, One God in Three Persons. ...
>
> Although I understand that, being God, He is
> happy in Himself and has absolutely no need of any
> creature, still, His goodness compels Him to give
> Himself to the creature, and with a generosity that is
> beyond understanding. ... Rejoice, all you creatures,
> for you are closer to God in His infinite mercy than
> a baby to its mother's heart.

In our day and age, many people tend to think of God's
act of 'creation' as something that happened billions of years
ago, when He brought the universe into being by the "Big
Bang" that allegedly started it all. Many also think of humanity
merely as the most recent product of some kind of process of
cosmic evolution. Wherever the truth may lie with regard to
these scientific theories about the past, however, Bl. Sopocko
points out that this is not the most meaningful aspect of God's
creation of the universe, and of the human race. The fact is
that nothing would exist from one moment to the next unless
God held all things in being at every moment. God first created
the universe long ago, but this does not mean that it had some
power to keep on existing on its own. Again, drawing on the
thought of St. Thomas Aquinas, Fr. Sopocko writes:

> All creatures not only receive existence from Him
> but also must be continuously sustained in their
> existence or determined to existence by Him. As
> the radiance of light from the sun is continually
> needed for daylight, so existence must constantly
> flow from God in order for creatures to exist. As
> a brook cannot flow unless the water comes from
> the source, so things cannot exist unless God
> gives and sustains their existence. Even angels and

human souls, although immortal in their nature, do not exist necessarily but need to be continuously conserved in being by the First Cause. If God did not pour existence constantly into His creatures, they would cease to exist and would return into nothingness (*God is Mercy*, chapter 13).

What all this means is clear enough: God literally loves us into being at every moment. Nobody is here by accident or merely by the working out of some random natural process. Nobody is cranked out by the universe in the way that a factory cranks out toys or toothpaste just because the machines were programmed to make such things from the beginning. Rather, each one of us springs fresh from our Creator's hands every day. To be sure, all this happens in accord with the patterns and laws of nature He established, but those "secondary causes" (that is, all creatures, and the natural properties that He gave to each of them) exist from moment to moment only because He wills to hold them in being, and thereby enables them to do what they do. In short, every single one of us is a continual "encore performance" of God's merciful love, a continual expression of His creative power and wisdom.

Saint Faustina echoes all this in her Canticle of Creation in her *Diary* (1750):

> Be adored, O our Creator and Lord.
> O universe, humbly glorify your God;
> Thank your Creator to the best of your powers
> And praise God's incomprehensible mercy. ...

> Come all you lovely things of earth,
> Which man does not cease to wonder at.
> Come, adore God in your harmony,
> Glorifying God's inconceivable mercy.

> Come, indelible beauty of all the earth,
> And with great humility adore your Creator,
> For all things are locked in His mercy,
> With one mighty voice all things cry out;
> How great is the mercy of God.

Chapter 9

MERCY OF GOD, INCONCEIVABLE MYSTERY OF THE HOLY TRINITY

Who ... will understand the mercies of the Lord?
— Psalm 106 [107]: 43

I. Like every free and rational being, God has His personality; that is, He possesses Himself and His nature as an independent being. He acts of Himself, with full consciousness, infinite authority, and unimpaired perfect right. Faith tells us that God differs from all other personal beings inasmuch as in Him is not only one Person, but three Persons, each having one common nature in His own specific manner. The Father possesses the divine nature, not being born and not descending from anyone. The Father [eternally] recognizes Himself and through this cognition He gives birth to an Image, living, perfect, and equal to Himself, and bestows on It His own divine nature. This Image is the Son of God, Who is begotten of the Father, or, in other words, arises from His reason and cognition and is, therefore, called the Wisdom and the Word of God. Since the Father and the Son possess the same nature, They know and love one another, and the manifestation of this Love is the Holy Spirit. The Father and the Son, through reciprocal Love, confer Their essence and nature on the third Divine Person for Him to possess. The Holy Spirit is this third Person. It is His property to proceed from the love of the Father and Son, and therefore He is called Love, Holiness, and the Gift, as the manifestation and result of their Love.

The Son of God, in the discourse at the Last Supper, promised the apostles the help of the Holy Spirit. On this occasion, He stated that not only would the Father send the Holy Spirit in the name of the Son, but He Himself would send the Spirit from the Father. Thus both together send the Spirit (Jn 15:26). This external statement, issued by Christ at a particular moment in created time, was only a manifestation of the interior eternal procession of the Divine Persons. The foundation of the teaching regarding the Holy Trinity is the firm irrevocable truth that there are no differences among the three Divine Persons other than the manner of their procession. All three Persons are one God, possessing one Nature, in which They reciprocally recognize and love each other. No one is able to comprehend the tenderness, the glowing love, and the supreme happiness with which the Father, from eternity, is always generating the Son, and the Holy Spirit proceeding from the Son and Father. All the brilliance, fire, and joy of the love that acts, enlivens, and inflames creatures is only a very weak reflection of the eternal generation of the Son by the Father and of the surge and procession of the Holy Spirit from the blazing Ocean of Divine Love that exists between the Father and the Son.

II. We know about the Holy Trinity only from divine revelation, since this truth is a mystery inaccessible to human reason. However, it is truly just and right for us to know everything that God has revealed, and especially to believe in the Holy Trinity since this is a condition of our salvation. God, in His infinite Mercy, has revealed some aspects of His unfathomable interior life to us. Therefore, it is fitting and necessary to listen to these revelations. Through His gift of allowing us to gaze into His most intimate life, He proves that He does not look upon us as servants and does not treat us as those who know nothing of what is happening in the bosom of their family, but He shows us that He acknowledges us as His children and friends before whom He has no secrets. The Savior manifested this attitude when He said, "No longer do I call you servants, because the servant does not know what his master does. But I have called you friends, because all things

that I have heard from My Father I have made known to you"
(Jn 15:15). Does this not give us reason to love God with
greater love, since He treats us with greater Mercy and more
like a father? For He shows us already something of His glory,
which one day we shall see when the veil is lifted in Heaven.
This is the great Mercy of God, which we should accept and for
which we should be grateful. Thus the devotion to the Mercy
of God is also devotion to the Holy Trinity and leads to a better
understanding of the Trinity through faith and love. It turns
our hearts to God, one in His Nature and infinitely Merciful,
as well as to the Divine Persons individually, demonstrating
the infinite Mercy in each Person, but especially in the Divine
Person of the Eternal Word Who has been made known to us
in the form of the God-Man Jesus Christ. In the Father are
manifested the eternity and majesty of God's Mercy; in the
Son the beauty and wisdom of this Mercy; and in the Holy
Spirit the goodness, love, joy, and happiness of this Mercy.
Each Person differs from the others, but is united to Them by
the proper relations existing between Them: i.e., the Father is
related to the Son by His Fatherhood, the Son to the Father
by His Sonship, and the Holy Spirit to the Father and Son by
the procession from both of Them. Each is like a link in a gold
chain, joined to each other.

*What a wonderful world of living harmony, peaceful
activity, communicative perfection, and differentiated
unity! This Ocean of power, love, and wisdom radiates
outwardly with beauty and with the charm of infinite
Mercy, which we should honor, but above all trust in!*

Chapter 10

MERCY OF GOD, EXPRESSION OF THE GREATEST POWER OF THE MOST HIGH

"The mercies of the Lord I will sing for ever"
— Psalm 88:2 [89:1]

I. The greatest power or Omnipotence of God consists in this, that He can do everything that is not in itself contradictory. Everything, regardless of how difficult or impossible it may seem to man, is possible for God provided it does not contain any internal contradiction. That, however, "which contains contradiction, cannot be a word, because reason can neither conceive nor express it" (St. Thomas Aquinas, *Summa Theologiae*, I, q.25, a.3).[19] Concerning the Omnipotence of God, Holy Scripture says, "for nothing shall be impossible with God" (Lk 1:37). In the Book of Wisdom, the Omnipotence of God is likened to His will. "But Thou being master of power, judgest with tranquility; and with great favor disposest of us; for Thy power is at hand when Thou wilt ... because in judging Thou givest place for repentance for sins" (Wis 12:18-19).

---

[19] What Bl. Sopocko — and St. Thomas Aquinas — mean here is that God cannot do things that involve a contradiction in terms (for example, He cannot create "a square circle" or "hatefully love us") not because there is any limitation on His omnipotence, but because these expressions have no real verbal content. C.S. Lewis once explained the matter like this:

> It remains true that all things are possible with God [Lk 1:37]... [but] it is no more possible for God than for the weakest of His creatures to carry out both of two mutually exclusive alternatives; not because His power meets an obstacle, but because nonsense remains nonsense even when we talk it about God (*The Problem of Pain*. New York: Touchstone, 1996 edition, p. 25).

If the power of God extends as far as His will does, and if His will is identical to His infinite being, then His power is infinite, and therefore God can do everything that is reasonable.

An act proper to Divine Omnipotence is imparting existence to nothingness, or creating. Creation is not a result of successive changes during a certain time but is achieved at one moment by God's creative act, which is both His will and His nature. As the true Master of all creatures, He showed Mercy by the very act of creating them, because He called them from nothingness into existence, although He was not compelled to do so.

Since the wretchedness of sin is far below nothingness, lifting a being up from this greatest misery and filling it with new holiness is therefore a manifestation of a power greater than creation.

The Mercy of God in Redemption is the greatest manifestation of His power, which pardons guilt and spares us punishment, through the infinite satisfaction for sin made by Jesus Christ. It precedes the justification of the sinner and incites him to conversion. It accompanies the sinner and all his endeavors to amend his life, and supports his weakness by the forgiveness of his guilt, the remission of punishment, and the infusion of grace into his soul. It arms the convert for the battle against temptations and directs him through works of penance to an attainment of the virtues he needs most. Finally, it endows him with the gifts of the Holy Spirit by which he is led to a participation in the Divine Life. Although God is able to punish sinners severely, or even annihilate them, He does not, but rather sustains them as if holding them in His own hand, nourishing them and filling them with pleasures, allowing the sun to shine and the rain to fall on them so that at the right moment He might forgive them, pour into them His love, and make them equal with the just. This is indeed the greatest manifestation of God's power.[20]

---

[20] By divine "power" here Bl. Sopocko seems to mean more than just God's ability to make everything happen the way He wants it to happen. God restrains that kind of all-determinative power (His "absolute will," in traditional terminology) in order

II. In his comment on the following passages in St. John's Gospel, "he who believes in Me, the works that I do, he also shall do, and greater than these he shall do" (Jn 14:12), St. Augustine sees in the expression "greater" the power of absolution, which the apostles and their successors received in order to justify the sinner. Considering this further, he adds, "It is easier to create the most perfect saints than to justify a sinner."

The Angelic Doctor, quoting the above sentence by St. Augustine, adds that God manifested greater power in redeeming the sinner through His infinite Mercy than in the creation of the most perfect heavenly spirits (*Summa Theologiae*, III, q. 43, a.4 and 2). Saint Hilary expresses the same idea by saying that it is greater to help others, and to forgive them their faults, than it is to punish them or create new beings.

Here can arise the difficulty of reconciling Mercy with eternal punishment. Saint Thomas clarifies this difficulty. Although the Mercy of God pities all, it regulates itself with eternal Wisdom, and does not reach those who reject Mercy in this life. It may be said that even the damned experience the Mercy of God, not in the sense that their punishment is shortened, but in the sense that their punishment is less intense than it should be in consideration of [the gravity of] the offenses committed.

We are all sinners, and we all experience the greatest power of God in our own justification. From sinners we become saints; from evildoers, workers of good; from sons of wrath, adopted children of God and heirs of His kingdom. "Give glory to the Lord, for He is good: for His Mercy endureth for ever" (Ps 105 [106]:1).

---

to make room for angelic and human free will (by His "permissive will"), that is, He gave to some of His creatures the ability to exercise voluntary agency and make real choices. By telling us that God's redemptive love is His greatest power, Bl. Sopocko seems to mean divine "power" here in the sense of the ability to achieve divine purpose. In whatever way angels and human beings use the freedom He gave to them, God is able to achieve through it all the manifestation of His great Mercy. And nothing manifests the great Wisdom of Divine Mercy more than His consummate skill in leading sinners home to His Merciful Heart.

Chapter 11

MERCY OF GOD, REVEALED IN THE CREATION OF THE HEAVENLY SPIRITS

"Their Angels in Heaven always behold the face of My Father in Heaven"
— Matthew 18:10

I. God first revealed His merciful Omnipotence in angelic, heavenly powers, which are first after God and which surround His throne. Saint Gregory of Nazianzus affirms (*Or.* 41, 11) that angels belong to a higher category of beings than man and their spirits mirror the image of Divinity. The understanding of their intellect is much more subtle, sharp, deep, and inclusive than ours, and their will is incomparably more perfect and stronger even in the conquest of matter than the greatest efforts of our strength and inventions. We read that one angel, with one blow, destroyed the whole army of Sennacherib (2 Macc 15:22).

Not all the angels are equal as to their kind and works. They differ externally through their offices and internally through their degrees of perfection and grace. According to St. Thomas, they are divided into three main categories. To the first category belong those who understand everything in great, general ideas; they are the created likeness of God's thought. To the second belong those who understand everything in the great laws and causes of nature. To the third belong those who understand everything through single ideas and particular causes (*Summa Theologiae*, I, q.108, aa.5 and 6). The seraphim, cherubim and thrones who form the first hierarchy are closest to God and are entrusted with serving

60

Him personally. The dominations, powers and virtues who form the second hierarchy take care of the world, through announcing God's decrees, quelling evil spirits, presiding over the order of the forces of nature, and occasionally suspending them through miracles. The principalities, archangels and guardian angels who form the third and lowest hierarchy are entrusted with the immediate care of people (countries; privileged and ordinary people). God always acts, whenever possible, through secondary causes (angels, etc.).

Marvelous, indeed splendid and wise, is the great heavenly structure in which each angel is a world complete in himself, and all of the angels together create a sequence of innumerable and increasingly more splendid hierarchies of knowledge, power, beauty, and holiness reaching the very steps of the throne of God's Majesty. By God's Mercy they were all raised to a supernatural state. Through humility, fidelity, and fortitude in the battle with the rebellious angels, they were confirmed in sanctity. They owe everything to God's Mercy, since of themselves they have merited nothing.

II. The creation of the heavenly spirits, and their endowment with such riches, is a manifestation of God's infinite Mercy toward man, because the angels purify, enlighten, and perfect our souls. Imagine how much Mercy God grants us through our guardian angels as referred to in Holy Scripture and Tradition. The Savior Himself says of children that their angels always see the face of the Father in Heaven. And why shouldn't this be applicable to all people? All human beings are surrounded with various dangers as regards soul and body, "For He hath given His angels charge over thee; to keep thee in all thy ways" (Ps 90 [91]:11). Angels surround people and nations, following them step by step; sharing in their joys, sufferings and needs; comforting them; caring for them; and giving them aid. Saint Paul writes that all the angels are ministering spirits "sent for service for the sake of those who shall inherit salvation" (Heb 1:14), which means that they protect us from the snares of the devils, pray for us, reprimand us and encourage us to do good, and carry our prayers and good works to God.

Who would not acknowledge the Mercy of God in the mediation of the angels on Mount Sinai (Acts 7:38 and 35); in their missions to Daniel (Dan 9:21) and to Mary (Lk 1:28); in the fulfillment of God's punishment on the persecutors of the Church, on such as Pharaoh and Herod (Acts 12:23), or on Heliodor (2 Macc 3:25); and in bestowing benefits on particular people (Tob 12:15) and on the Church (Acts 12:7)?

"Their angels see the face of My Merciful Father" [Mt 18:10], and this vision encourages them to work indefatigably on our behalf. The face of God is Mercy Itself. The angels see God's concern for us in the gifts He showers on us, in the golden net of His love by which He ensnares us, in His anticipation of our goodwill and the grateful acceptance of it. For these reasons the angels are ever ready to serve us, and through this service they are drawn into the orbit of God's infinite Mercy, which is shown to us.

I will consider this deeply, and I will adore God's Mercy in my guardian angel, loving, obeying, and venerating him daily. I will put my trust in his protection.

Chapter 12

MERCY OF GOD, SUMMONING US TO EXISTENCE OUT OF NOTHINGNESS

"The spirit of God made me, and the breath
of the Almighty gave life"
— Job 33:4

I. Creation seems to be a work of the Goodness of God. As from a full vessel the contents tend to be poured out, so the Eternal Goodness of His perfect fullness tends to communicate Itself to others, and this Goodness, therefore, is the chief motive of creation.

However, God's natural goodness sufficiently manifests itself in the Holy Trinity, in the eternal generation of the Son by the Father and in the procession of the Holy Spirit from the Father and Son, and in the mutual love of the three Divine Persons. Here is poured out all the fullness of the most perfect natural goodness of God. Through this, its tendency to communicate itself to others is fully satisfied. The creation of the rational world was not necessary to express God's goodness, since God has always been happy in Himself and entirely self-sufficient. Therefore, creation happened without any external or internal compulsion, without necessity, but only through the infinite Mercy of God. In regard to miseries and deficiencies, which are an indispensable condition for exercising Mercy, these may be understood more generally. Lack of existence, or nothingness, is the greatest of all wants and the most extreme misery. All nature shudders before such misery. Every animal, and every human being, flees from this want, fearing it above all other sufferings and wants, proving thus that lack of existence is the greatest of all miseries. So creation of the world with all its beings is the work of the Mercy of God, which may also be called Divine Goodness in relation to this supreme misery of nonexistence.[21]

II. Holy Scripture expressly teaches us in many instances that God created the world out of His Mercy. "All the ways of the Lord are Mercy" (Ps 24 [25]:10), says the psalmist. Since he refers to all external works of the Lord, creation is also a result of the infinite Mercy of God. Thus he points out that Mercy is found in every act of God toward His creatures. It is in Psalm 135 that the inspired singer calls the various works of God the works of His Mercy and, among them, He gives first place to the creation of the world: "Praise the Lord, for He is good: for His Mercy endureth for ever. ... Who established the earth above the waters: for His Mercy endureth for ever. Who made the great lights: for His Mercy endureth for ever. The sun to rule the day: for His Mercy endureth for ever" (Ps 135 [136]:1 and 6-8). The sense of these words is very clear; it is the litany of the Mercy of God in the work of creation.

---

[21] [From the 1965 edition] Saint Thomas Aquinas expressly teaches that Divine Mercy was manifested in the creation of the world. In his *Commentary on the Four Books of Peter Lombard's Sentences*, Distincio XVI, Quaestio II, art. II, he puts forth the following objection: "It seems that God's Mercy and Justice do not appear here because the work of creation does not presuppose anything. Now, the work of justice presupposes a debt; and work of mercy presupposes misery. Therefore, Justice and Mercy cannot be in the work of creation."

Saint Thomas's answer is:

[J]ustice sometimes consists in the retribution of things which are merited; in such a case one cannot consider justice in the creation. However, Justice consists sometimes in an act which is fitting to Divine Goodness; in such a case Justice does not presuppose anything on the part of the one benefited, but only on the part of God. Thus, Justice can be present in the work of creation, but only on the part of God. Thus, Justice can be present in the work of creation for it is just that each thing have its being in such a way as it is preordained by Divine Wisdom.

Likewise, mercy has two meanings. In one sense, it is the removal of a previous misery by one who is not obliged to do so; in such a case Mercy is present in the work of creation, for God, in the act of creation removes the greatest defect, namely, nothingness; moreover, since He is not compelled to it by anything. He does so gratuitously.

The creation of humanity in the image and likeness of God is a very special work of the Divine Mercy. Human beings differ from other visible creatures in that each of us possesses a rational soul, and thus joins in himself two worlds: material and spiritual. It is above all else the spirituality of the invisible soul with its two main faculties, reason and free will, that makes us the image and likeness of God. Besides, as a representative of the material world humanity subdues the gigantic inorganic, vegetative, and animal kingdoms to God. Therefore we may rightly say that human beings are the masterpiece of creation, a wonder of the infinite Mercy of God, a small world in ourselves, a microcosm, as humanity was called by ancient philosophers.[22]

We have every reason to regard the Merciful Creator with the deepest gratitude and with childlike trust. We bear His image in ourselves, and all that we have and are comes from Him. We have nothing that has not been given us by Him, that He does not consider His own, that has not been embraced by His Mercy. "Praise the Lord, for He is good: for His Mercy endureth for ever."

---

[22] By "microcosm" here, Bl. Sopocko is referring to the teaching of the Fathers of the Church, such as St. Maximus the Confessor, that human beings sum up the whole creation in themselves, because they include every level of created being in their own: the material, vegetative, animal, and spiritual levels of created being, all rolled into one.

COMMENTARY:
THE MERCIFUL GOD LOOKS
AFTER US DAY BY DAY

Many people see their lives as little more than an endless string of sufferings and frustrations. As Henry David Thoreau once wrote, most human beings lead lives of "quiet desperation." Blessed Sopocko assures us, however, that they have been deceived: God is not asleep! He is at work in your life and mine, if only we have eyes to see, and He will work even more powerfully in our lives than we can ask or imagine if only we open our hearts to Him in prayer, and put all our trust in His merciful love. His providential care extends to all of creation and especially to human beings, whom He made in His own image and bought with the price of His own blood.

Father Sopocko reminds us of these truths in his book *God is Mercy*, again and again:

> It is ... our Savior who stresses Mercy in the Divine Providence, which takes care, not only of human beings, but also of the most [lowly] things such as sparrows and the lilies of the field. Therefore, He forbids us to worry excessively about temporal goods: "Do not be anxious for your life, what you shall eat: nor yet for your body, what you shall put on ... for your Father knows that you need all these things" (Mt 6:26-32). ... [A]bove everything else God in His Mercy wants to take care of His creatures, so that they might reach their goal [that is, eternal life]. This motive seems to be dominant and decisive in the Providence of God (*God is Mercy*, chapter 13).

We need to understand what Bl. Sopocko means by "the Providence of God." It is not a pious platitude; it is also not an expression of a "sugary sweet" kind of spirituality in which we delude ourselves that if we prayerfully entrust our lives to our Lord, He will ensure that we never have to feel deep sorrow or experience terrible suffering. If the Cross was the path to Heaven for our Lord and Savior, how could it be any different for all who seek to follow Him? Jesus said: "If any man would come after Me, let him deny himself, and take up his cross and follow Me" (Mt 16:24).

In fact, as Bl. Sopocko points out, some crosses of sadness are actually good for us to carry, because they purify our hearts and draw us nearer to God. Most of all, he focuses on contrition for sin, compassion for the suffering, and longing for union with God:

> The right kind of sadness comes from God. It is caused by the realization of our own misery, a recognition of our sins, compassion for the physical and spiritual misfortunes of others, our longing for God, and the thought that God is offended. The fruit of this sadness is the purification of the heart, abundant merit, and holy solace. "Blessed are they who mourn, for they shall be comforted" (Mt 5:4). (*God is Mercy*, chapter 33)

As Bl. Sopocko teaches, our compassion for the plight of others can be expressed by praying for their needs, by words of love, and by deeds of mercy. Our longing for God can be assuaged by our drawing near to Him in prayer and the Sacraments. But of all our sorrows, the sadness in our hearts caused by repentance is perhaps dearest to our Savior's Heart. Commenting on our Lord's parable of the Good Shepherd in Luke 15:6 ("Rejoice with me, because I have found my sheep that was lost"), Bl. Sopocko writes:

> Who would believe that the Lord ... has His days of special joy on which He seems to be more happy than usual? When does the Lord feel such joy? Is it when people render Him glory, when they build

sanctuaries to Him, when the martyrs give their life
for His Name? No doubt, God rejoices in all that.
But the summit of His joy is the conversion of the
sinner. It is the day of gladness for God when the
sinful man abandons his sordid life and washes
himself with tears of sorrow for having offended
God; when the extortioner, the usurer, and the
wrongdoer stop their malice and, like Zacheus,
compensate [their victims] in a fourfold manner
for the wrongs committed against them; when the
fickle and fallen woman rises from her degradation
and, like Magdalen, becomes a penitent; when any
sinner amends his way of life (*God is Mercy*, chapter 29).

Sometimes our sadness is caused not by any of these
three good things (that is, by our compassion for others,
contrition for sin, or longing for God) but simply by our
bodily weaknesses, such as emotional or physical exhaustion,
serious illness, or grief at the loss of loved ones. But the Good
Shepherd has numerous ways of reaching out to us to refresh
us on our journey, and to lighten these burdens on our road
to Heaven. Blessed Sopocko shows us how tenderly to care
for ourselves and others when we are weighed down with
such sorrows:

Sometimes sadness is a symptom of a tendency
to disease or a direct effect of actual disease. In
this case one should undergo medical treatment,
and use exterior means like reading good books,
or gazing at a beautiful countryside. A change of
abode, singing, and the company of dear friends are
efficacious too, but the most efficacious means is
the company of our best friend, the Merciful Jesus,
Who applies balm soothing all the wounds of the
human heart (*God Is Mercy*, chapter 33).

Chapter 13

MERCY OF GOD,
EMBRACING THE WHOLE UNIVERSE

*"She (Wisdom) reacheth therefore from
end to end mightily, and ordereth all
things sweetly [mercifully]"*
— Wisdom 8:1

I. All creatures are always absolutely dependent on the Creator, Who alone is Being Itself in His very nature. All creatures not only receive existence from Him, but also must be continuously sustained in their existence or determined to existence by Him. As the radiance of light from the sun is continually needed for daylight, so existence must constantly flow from God in order for creatures to exist. As a brook cannot flow unless the water comes from the source, so things cannot exist unless God gives and sustains their existence. Even angels and human souls, although immortal in their nature, do not exist necessarily but need to be continuously conserved in being by the First Cause. If God did not pour existence constantly into His creatures, they would cease to exist and would return to nothingness (*Summa Theologiae*, I, q. 104, a. 3).

Moreover, God cooperates in all acts of creatures (*concursus*). With respect to the moral value of an act He influences creatures solely as they do good works; with respect to the physical side of an act He supplies His creatures with the power and means to do this act and also naturally and universally assists creatures in the very deed. God and the creatures cooperate in the same act, hence this act proceeds from God, Who not only imparts the power but energizes it; and from the created agent, which under the divine influences uses its God-given power. "Lord, Thou wilt give us peace: for Thou hast wrought all our works for us" (Is 26:12), says the prophet, pointing out that even though acts come from created causes, they also come from God.

God not only sustains every creature in existence and cooperates naturally in its acts, but also assigns it a proper end and suitable means to bring it to this end. We call this end and the means leading to it Divine Providence. General Providence embraces all creatures without exception. God "made the little and the great, and he hath equally care of all" (Wis 6:8). Only certain people experience exceptional Providence. As to a few chosen ones, they are surrounded with extraordinary Providence. The facts that the Holy Scriptures relate about Joseph, Moses, Abraham, David, Tobias, Peter in prison, etc., are proof of extraordinary Providence.

II. The conservation of the world; cooperation with creatures; and Divine Providence, general and exceptional, are manifestations of the infinite Mercy of God. This is said by the inspired psalmist attributing the conservation of all living beings to God's Mercy: "Who giveth food to all flesh: for His Mercy endureth for ever" (Ps 135 [136]:25). It is confirmed by the author of the Book of Wisdom, who refers to God as the Merciful Father Whose Providence governs all: "Thy Providence, O Father, governeth it" (Wis 14:3).

It is, however, our Savior Who stresses Mercy in the Divine Providence, which takes care, not only of human beings, but also of the most lowly things such as sparrows and the lilies of the field. Therefore, He forbids us to worry excessively about temporal goods: "Do not be anxious for your life, what you shall eat: nor yet for your body, what you shall put on ... for your Father knows that you need all these things" (Mt 6:25-32). God in His wisdom assigns a suitable end to creatures as well as the means leading to it. God in His Omnipotence can bring about all that He proposes Himself. However, above everything else God in His Mercy wants to take care of His creatures so that they might reach their goal [that is, eternal life]. This motive seems to be dominant and decisive in the Providence of God.

Every detail of the visible world witnesses the merciful protection exercised by God; all beings proclaim with the inspired author of Wisdom, "Thou lovest all things that are" (Wis 11:25), with the love of a Superior Being for lower beings, which love is Mercy. The visible world exists for man, whom God has instituted as king and lord of all beings on earth. Therefore, man, above all other creatures, is the object of the special care of the Merciful Creator. The best proof of this may be found in the life of each of us. Should we look carefully into the vicissitudes of our life, we would discover many an event in which the watchfulness of God's Mercy is manifested to us. No wonder that the first thought born in us with respect to God is the recognition of His Mercy, because everyone knows it clearly from personal experience. This is the child's first word, the first exclamation of its reason.

Let us often repeat with the psalmist, "Thy Mercy is before my eyes: and I am well pleased with Thy truth" (Ps 25 [26]:3).

Chapter 14

MERCY OF GOD, BESTOWING UPON US IMMORTAL LIFE

"According to His great Mercy (God)
has begotten us again ... unto a living hope"
— 1 Peter 1:3

I. The human being as a rational animal is the head of all non-rational creatures, and God has endowed him with an immortal soul: "And the Lord God formed man of the slime of the earth: and breathed into his face the breath of life, and man became a living soul" (Gen 2:7).

All nations of the world have always believed and continue to believe in the immortality of the human soul. This belief must be true, because all of humanity cannot err universally on such a vital question.[23] We all seek the truth and desire perfect happiness, which cannot be found on earth. Because our desires demand a proper end, this desire cannot be in vain but must be able to find satisfaction after death in life everlasting. The purely spiritual activities of the human soul are intangible and inaccessible to matter or our organic faculties: for instance, [knowledge of] general and purely spiritual concepts (spirit, God, good, properties, law) and the logical relation between concepts and judgments, reflection on one's own thought and desires, special qualities of speech,

---

[23] In light of contemporary scholarship since Bl. Sopocko wrote these words, it would probably be more accurate to say that many of the world's civilizations and religions have believed in at least some kind of immortality. The desire to transcend death, therefore, is nearly universal, even if not always expressed in the form of a belief in "the immortality of the soul."

progress, morals, religion and free will.[24] Moreover, only that which does not exist in itself (the color of a flower), or that which decomposes into parts (material things) can perish. However, the soul neither consists of parts into which it could decompose, nor grows old in its activities. "In the ancient is wisdom, and in length of days prudence" (Job 12:12). Holy Scripture distinguishes the soul from the body, and says that when man dies, his body will turn into ashes and his soul shall return to God, its Creator. "Remember thy Creator in the days of thy youth before ... the dust return into its earth from whence it was and the spirit return to God, Who gave it" (Eccl 12:1 and 7). One can kill the body but not the soul. "And do not be afraid of those who kill the body but cannot kill the soul" (Mt 10:28). To the Good Thief, who was soon to die on a cross, Christ said, "This day thou shalt be with Me in paradise" (Lk 23:43). Obviously, these words applied to his soul, because his body remained on earth. "He who loves his life, loses it; and he who hates his life in this world, keeps it unto life everlasting" (Jn 12:25). From the above text and arguments of Holy Writ we see that the soul, after death, exists independently of matter, that it suffers or rejoices according to its merits on earth, and that it lives eternally.

II. Moreover, by immortal life, or life everlasting, Holy Scripture understands a state of sanctifying grace and supernatural happiness after death. God, in His infinite Mercy, saw innumerable shortcomings of human nature, which made man miserable, and so He deigned to provide him with perfections, which were not due to his nature, but were supernatural, and these were to be imparted only by grace. These perfections are justification and holiness, otherwise called sanctifying grace, which like a special garment makes us just and holy before God. With such a garment God clothed our first parents in paradise, and because of this

---

[24] Blessed Sopocko's point here is that all these operations of a human mind cannot be attributed merely to physical or organic processes (for example, to the working of the human brain alone). Thus, they show that each human being possesses not only a material, organic body, but also an immaterial, spiritual soul.

their souls became beautiful, resembling the angels. With this grace, from ordinary creatures they became children of God and subjects of the particular favor and love of the Creator, Who treated them as the father of a family would treat his children. Through this grace they acquired the right to enter Heaven and to see God face to face in the beatific vision and participate in His life, happiness, and glory. Besides this, they also received preternatural gifts such as infused knowledge, interior harmony of affections and faculties of the soul, freedom from suffering and from miseries, and above all, the immortality of the body in addition to that of the soul. They were never to die. These supernatural and preternatural gifts (with the exception of knowledge) were to descend on all people. The preternatural gifts were given to shield and guard sanctifying grace, so that the loss of sanctifying grace caused by sin resulted also in the loss of the preternatural gifts.

God made humanity holy by giving us sanctifying grace, but in Scripture holiness is often called justice, which is usually mentioned side by side with Mercy: "Mercy and truth have met each other: justice and peace have kissed" (Ps 84:11 [85:10]). Hence we see that the supernatural state of our first parents, and the calling of all people to this state, is a work of God's infinite Mercy, which destines us to a life of eternal happiness.

We see, then, that God endowed human beings with the immortal life of the soul (natural immortality). Since we in no way merited this favor, we must attribute it to Divine Mercy. However, the deepest aspiration of humanity was for a still fuller life, an immortal life of both soul and body in eternal happiness. Christ gave the answer to this longing. "He who eats Me, he also shall live because of Me" (Jn 6:58).

Although I will esteem natural immortality highly, yet with still greater attention will I aspire to supernatural immortality, which I can recover by the grace of the Most Merciful Savior given in the Sacraments of Baptism and Penance, and which I keep alive by receiving the Sacrament of the Altar frequently.

Chapter 15

MERCY OF GOD, SHIELDING US FROM PUNISHMENTS

"The Just Man shall correct me in Mercy"
— Psalm 140 [141]:5

I. A law without sanction is not real, and points to the imprudence of the lawgiver. This cannot be so with God, Who, already in the Garden of Eden, announced the punishment for transgressing His law: "in what day soever thou shalt eat of it [the tree], thou shalt die the death" (Gen 2:17). Death, therefore, is punishment for sin. Thus original sin resulted in the loss of temporal and eternal life. In this very announcement of punishment, the great Mercy of God, which did not demand eternal damnation, is already manifested. This Mercy, however, was shown in a still higher degree, since the punishment it exacted was infinitely smaller than the guilt. If God were guided by Justice alone, He might have annihilated the first human beings immediately after the first sin, or at least have condemned them forever, as He did the rebellious angels. However, in having sentenced them to sufferings and temporal death only, He did not take away from us the immortality of the soul, but even promised a Redeemer Who would bestow supernatural and everlasting happiness on those who would believe in Him, and in the end He would even restore life to the body through resurrection. The words of the prophet, "The Just Man shall correct me in Mercy," were verified already in paradise.

In the Scriptures we see that God continually exacted punishment mercifully. He shielded people from penalties due to actual sin when, on account of their faith in the coming Redeemer, He freed repentant sinners from eternal punishment, and in meting out temporal punishment He aimed first of all at their amendment. Even the Deluge had the characteristics of a remedy in the punishment, because, according to the testimony of St. Peter, facing the threat of death, many sinners were converted to God and instead of going to hell, they reached Purgatory, whence our Savior liberated them (1 Pet 3:19-22). If it was like this in the Old Testament, the Testament of Law, it is even more so in the New Testament, the Testament of Grace. The Redeemer protects us from well-deserved punishments. First of all, He frees us from eternal punishment through the Sacraments of Baptism and Penance. Then He facilitates our liberation from temporal punishment by establishing the treasury of His merits, from which the Church draws and distributes indulgences. "God Who is rich in Mercy ... when we were dead by reason of our sins, brought us to life together with Christ" (Eph 2:4 and 5).

II. "The earth, O Lord, is full of Thy Mercy: teach me Thy justification" (Ps 118 [119]:64), says the psalmist. This means that Divine Mercy manifests itself even in temporal punishments, and thus in the future life protects us from eternal penalties, which we justly incur by our mortal sins. The Mercy of God, however, does not mean complete impunity. Like the manna in the desert it flows for a limited time, and after this it will forever cease to flow. Prior to the awful punishment of the Deluge the time of Divine Mercy was extended over a period of 120 years (Gen 6:3), but for the Ninevites it lasted only 40 days (Jon 3:4).

To every one of us there is assigned a moment of mercy and penance for sins; woe to the soul that does not heed this time of God's Mercy. According to the warning of the prophet, "Hasten to take away the spoils; make haste to take the prey" (Is 8:3). Let us hasten while the heavens are brightened with the clement weather of pity, before it covers itself with the clouds of justice and wrath.

Though people often do not fully appreciate the meaning of the phrase, "temporal spiritual punishments," these are a commencement of the eternal ones after death. They consist in depriving us of a fourfold spiritual good in this life — sanctifying grace, interior impulses or inspirations toward good, spiritual direction, and a safeguard from falls into sin. We have great difficulty in discerning spiritual things, and for this reason we need an interior impulse and the enlightenment of our mind not only momentarily, but continually. Spiritual direction consists in the removal of obstacles and in the provision of occasions and salutary advice to enable the performance of meritorious acts, such as entering the religious state. Safeguarding us from falls consists in the subjugation of Satan's power, the ability to turn away from temptations and perilous occasions and to receive interior aid in overcoming them. In consequence of our infidelities, God lessens and withdraws from the soul these interior aids, but in this life we are never entirely deprived of Divine Mercy. If only we cooperate with it, we shall surely be converted to God.

I thank You, O Lord, for supporting me so many times in spite of my infidelities. Wherever I ran in my blindness, there, swift-winged in pursuit, Your Mercy came to me. Help me to profit always by every moment of grace.

Chapter 16

MERCY OF GOD, RAISING US FROM THE MISERY OF SIN

"Many are the scourges of the sinner, but Mercy shall encompass him that hopeth in the Lord"
— Psalm 31 [32]:10

I. Sin is the greatest misery in itself and in the effects that it causes. There is great stupidity in every sin (according to the philosopher Boethius), for sin is unreasonable conduct motivated by animal passion, an inhuman act.

Sin is an offense against God, an infinite evil on account of the infinite dignity of the One offended and the infinite misery of the offender. Sin is arrogance in the eyes of God, Who always sees the sinner through the eyes of a witness and a judge.[25] "I am the judge and the witness, saith the Lord" (Jer 29:23). Sin is the placing of the created above the Creator; "there is a deceitful balance in his hand" (Hos 12:7). Sin is an attempt at deicide, which actually took place on Golgotha. Every sinner strives anew to crucify Christ, in Whom "there is Mercy: and with Him plentiful redemption" (Ps 129 [130]:7).

The effects of sin in the soul and in the body of a human being are truly horrible. A mortal sin strips him of sanctifying grace and deprives him of the dignity of being a child of God and instead makes him Satan's child. "He who does not love

---

[25] What Bl. Sopocko means here, of course, is that God is just, and also omniscient; He sees all things, and is aware of all things, so that nothing escapes His attention. Blessed Sopocko does not mean that God is like a celestial policeman who is constantly keeping an eye on us in order to catch us in some sin if He can. Precisely because God is aware of our sin, He pursues us with His mercy to heal and forgive us, to restore us to wholeness and holiness.

abides in death" (1 Jn 3:14). Moreover, [mortal] sin deprives the sinner of his old merits and renders him unable to acquire any new ones. It causes anxiety and remorse of conscience and leads to eternal rejection and damnation.

No less horrible are the effects of sin in temporal life: diseases, with the most painful sufferings; wars, with the most dismal consequences; hunger, affliction, despair, and countless other sorrows; and the end of all this, death. The history of humanity is a history of sin, a ceaseless painful groan. It is a display of calamities and punishments, a continual drama of crime resulting from the drama of sin. "Depart from me, you workers of iniquity" (Mt 7:23).

II. "I have blotted out thy iniquities as a cloud, and thy sins as a mist" (Is 44:22), says God through the mouth of the prophet announcing the coming Redeemer. In His turn the Redeemer proclaims, "I desire Mercy and not sacrifice. For I have come to call sinners, not the just" (Mt 9:13). Here the Mercy of God does not stand in opposition to Justice but surpasses it. Instead of crushing the sinner with a just vengeance for his iniquity, Mercy makes him contrite with humility. Instead of burdening him with due punishment, it moves him with the sorrow of contrition. And if blood is needed to satisfy Justice, then Mercy does it with the infinite satisfaction of the Blood of the God-Man.[26] In this Blood are manifest the infinite wretchedness of sin and God's irrevocable Justice, but above all, His infinite Mercy. In Christ dying on the Cross, "Mercy and truth have met each other: justice and peace have kissed" (Ps 84:11 [85:10]).

If the merits of all the saints and heavenly spirits together with those of the Blessed Virgin Mary were put on one scale, and only one mortal sin on the other, undoubtedly this sin alone would outweigh all those merits, since they, however great they might be, will always be finite and insufficient to satisfy the infinite offenses given to God's Majesty by only

---

[26] On a similar use of traditional theological language by Bl. Sopocko, see note 15, above.

one mortal sin. Through the infinite Mercy of God, Christ the Redeemer made a worthy payment for sin and raised up from the misery of sin all who would believe in Him, and who reasonably avail themselves of the means of salvation. "But if any one sins, we have an advocate with the Father, Jesus Christ the just, and He is the propitiation for our sins, not for ours only, but also for those of the whole world" (1 Jn 2:1-2); that is to say, one drop of the Blood of the God-Man outweighs the sins of the whole world.[27]

> I shall meditate on the efficacy and the never-weakening force of Christ's Blood, which contains the weight of eternal glory and through which the Divine power elevates and raises us up from the greatest sins. "His Blood gives color to my countenance," says St. Agnes. This Blood should color my face also.[28]

---

[27] Saint Faustina also believed that the value of each of the sufferings of Christ, out of love for us, was more than enough to make up for the sins of the whole world. See *Diary*, 72.

[28] Blessed Sopocko seems to mean here that repentant and faithful Christians should always see themselves as sinners for whom Christ shed His blood, and whose sins have been washed away by the Blood of the Lamb.

COMMENTARY:
THE MERCIFUL GOD BECAME FLESH
AND DIED FOR US ON THE CROSS

Life can be brutal at times. For all the goodness in God's creation, there are many experiences in life — sickness, accidents, disease, and death — of nature's seeming indifference to human happiness and, beyond that, of "man's inhumanity to man" (e.g., murder and theft, adultery and apostasy, war and injustice, lies and deceit). In short, God may be "loving us into being" at every moment, as previously discussed, but the kind of world in which we live often does not seem to manifest the mercy of God at all.

Blessed Michael Sopocko was well aware of this. While he accepted the traditional proofs for the existence of God drawn from the philosophy of St. Thomas Aquinas, he also knew that human vision is clouded by sin and suffering, and cannot see the truth for what it is. Out of His merciful love for us, therefore, God pierced through the darkness and sent us the light of His Son:

> Human reason can have knowledge of God by observing the visible things of nature, but, on account of original sin, it attains truth only imperfectly and with great difficulty, especially the ultimate Truth — God. It was fitting, then, that God should become Man in order to permit human beings to know Him more easily. *In the person of Jesus Christ, God reveals Himself to the people.* ... "Philip, he who sees Me sees also the Father" (Jn 14:9). ... He revealed to us the unfathomable perfections of God, and through this made it possible for us to know and to love God, and made us His

brothers and sisters, as well as adopted children of
God (*God is Mercy*, chapter 1).

Blessed Sopocko repeatedly points out the reason why
God is so clearly revealed to us in Jesus Christ: because Jesus
is the Divine Son, the "Word" (or self-expression) of God in
human flesh. After all, who can reveal to us the merciful Heart
of God the Father more clearly than God the Son dwelling
among us, and sharing with us all of the joys, sorrows, and
sufferings of the human journey?

Blessed Sopocko also repeatedly asks us to meditate on
the most stupendous demonstration of God's merciful love
for us during the life of His Son on earth: namely, Christ's
agony, Passion, and death. He writes:

> The greatest evidence of God's Mercy is that his
> Son found a means unheard of, unique, unfailing,
> inconceivable, worthy of admiration and ecstatic
> praise. He resolved to take our human nature, so
> that in and through it He might reform human
> nature and bring salvation to all of humanity. Only
> He, since He was equal to God the Father, and at
> the same time a man, could give God's Majesty
> worthy satisfaction for the offense of original and
> actual sin, and establish a treasury, from which in
> the future it would be possible to draw continually
> in reparation for sin. ... Our Savior chose the most
> painful kind of death [death on a cross] in order that
> He might make satisfaction to the Divine Justice for
> our sins and provide for us as ransom the frightful
> pains on the cross as evidence of His Mercy (*God is
> Mercy*, chapters 7 and 18).

As Catholics we often repeat the slogan "Jesus died for
our sins" without stopping to think what this really means.
In the quotation above, Bl. Sopocko has summed up for us
in a nutshell the mystery of the Cross: God loved the world
so much that He was determined to lift from our shoulders

the burden of guilt that we carry because of our sins. We know very well we deserve divine punishment for our moral failings, and in fact we often punish ourselves, and others, with destructive behavior as a result. Only the Merciful God Himself, in human flesh, could take on our behalf the penalty that our sins deserve. In fact, His Passion and death on the Cross more than made up for our debt to Divine Justice. As Fr. Sopocko said, it gained for us a whole "treasury" of merits and graces that we can draw upon at any time, through repentance, faith, and the Sacraments. In short, God did not just balance the books by taking the rap for our sins on the Cross; He also merited a whole ocean of graces for those who are willing to open their hearts to Him in repentance and trust.

Do we really appreciate what a gift of merciful love it is for us to live on this side of Good Friday? Even God's Chosen People, the ancient Jews, who frequently extolled the mercy of God in their Scriptures, really had no idea that God's mercy could go as far as Gethsemane and Calvary. According to Bl. Sopocko, Christians are privileged to live in the light that shines on us from the Incarnation and the Cross:

> [W]e are indebted to God's Mercy for being born, not in pre-Christian times when there was a dearth of the heavenly gifts, but even now, in the golden age of grace. The Merciful Jesus preceded us with graces and created our souls when Satan was already defeated, death conquered, Heaven opened, Divine Mercy revealed, and the straight road to Heaven clearly shown. Truly, this is the golden age of grace, since at any time the sinner can easily repair the faults of His whole life. Divine Mercy descends on us more plentifully than snowflakes in the winter. ... We have, by God's Mercy, received Baptism in His Church, learned the principles of the true faith, and profited by the means of sanctification (*God is Mercy*, chapter 28).

Thus whenever we are weighed down by a burden of suffering, or by the burden of our sins, we have only to turn to the Cross to find reassurance that the God who loved us so much that He was even willing to die for us will never abandon us. As Jesus said to St. Faustina:

My mercy is greater than your sins, and those of the entire world. Who can measure the extent of my goodness? For you I descended from heaven to earth; for you I allowed myself to be nailed to the cross; for you I let my Sacred Heart be pierced with a lance, thus opening wide the source of mercy for you. Come, then, with trust, to draw graces from this fountain. I never reject a contrite heart. Your misery has disappeared in the depths of My mercy (*Diary*, 1485).

Chapter 17

MERCY OF GOD, JUSTIFYING US IN THE WORD INCARNATE

"The Word was made flesh"
— John 1:14

I. In the Incarnation of the eternal Word, the Redemption or the justification of the human race was accomplished in a most suitable way, a way most corresponding to the Wisdom, Power, Justice, and above all Mercy of God. Divine Power manifests itself to us in the working of miracles, and Divine Wisdom in the choice of the means most proper to the most sublime end. It is in the Incarnation that we see a most sublime end, the elevation of human nature to divine nature. As a means to this end God chose the union of divine nature with human nature in one Person, Christ, by the hypostatic union. What can be more and more worthy of admiration than that the Son of God, never ceasing to be God, should become human? That in one and the same Person He should unite all that is divine and human, the human body with its senses and passions, human reason and will with the divine reason and will and with all the divine perfections?

Here we see not only that God gives man His grace, but that He unites Himself with humankind in the plentitude of His divinity in the one Divine Person. Divine Justice manifests itself through the Incarnation, since in this way the offense against the Infinite Majesty is most effectively atoned for. It is not a mere creature but the God-Man Who makes satisfaction. In the Incarnation is revealed the infinite wretchedness of sin, which the Son of God came to wipe out. The Redemption of humanity from slavery to the devil was achieved through the Incarnation. Lucifer was not entirely deprived of the powers of a higher spirit, and only at the price of the Blood of the God-Man was his power over human beings checked.

But above all else, the Mercy of God is revealed in the Incarnation, since by no other gift could God so clearly manifest His pity for man as in giving him His Only Begotten Son. Over and above this gift there is nothing of greater value or efficacy for our salvation. The gratuitous forgiveness of our sins or atonement by means of some creature, even the most perfect, would not be a justification and would not reveal as much Mercy as is revealed in the adequate and just satisfaction made by God's most beloved Son. Finally, the mystery of the Incarnation has established an everlasting font of salvation, ever actively washing away our sins. "You have been bought at a great price" (1 Cor 6:20).

II. The manner of uniting two natures in one person surpasses the comprehension of men and angels. Only [divine] revelation, then, teaches us that in Christ the complete human nature communicates its properties to the eternal Word, and that He in turn communicates His divine properties to human nature. The Person of Christ dominates the two natures and acts through each of these as if through one. Just as God united the human body to the soul through which the body becomes spiritualized, beautified, enlivened, and a partaker of the honors of the soul, so likewise in the second Person of the Holy Trinity, divine nature unites itself to the human, in order to ennoble, adorn, and vivify it with a new life, and thus deifies it.[29] Divine nature does not lower itself or change

---

[29] Blessed Sopocko follows the classical tradition of Catholic Christology, which holds that in the Incarnation we have one Divine Person, the second Person of the Holy Trinity, in two natures: in other words, without ceasing to be fully divine, the eternal Son of God came to dwell among us in a fully human way. As a result of this unique union in Him between divinity and humanity, it was said, the divine Son's human nature must have received a radiation of supernatural life and light from His divine nature (e.g., see Jn 1:14, which tells us that Jesus Christ was "full of grace and truth"), so that even His human flesh was healing and life-giving (e.g., Lk 8:43-48), and from infancy His human mind enjoyed the beatific vision, and the fullness of

because of this union, but human nature is raised to divine dignity like an earthly twig grafted into a heavenly vine. Just as the sun's rays passing through air illumine it, warm it, and fill it with sunshine, so the Son of God, by taking on human nature, clothes it with the same splendor with which He Himself shines, as was manifested in the Transfiguration on Mount Tabor. Humanity becomes at the same time a natural Son of God, for human nature exists in the Person of the Son of God. By the fact that one human being became a natural Son of God, God the Father adopted as His children all who would believe in the Son. This sole natural Son of God took flesh from the Most Pure Virgin, who became the Mother of Mercy for all the adopted children of God, and Mediatrix of all graces that flow from God to them.

The benefits of Incarnation are unlimited. For the gift of this Incarnation is not a most perfect angel, but God's Son, Whom the Heavenly Father has given us as our possession solely for our good. Not only were all the graces restored that had been lost by sin, but, in addition, our Savior merited for humanity an infinite treasure of merits, from which we are always able to draw abundantly. "Glory to God in the highest; and on earth peace" (Lk 2:14). Peace is not punishment and death, but mercy, pardon, and justification for "men of good will," who in all humility shall trust in the Incarnate Word and recognize in Him the Son of God.

I discern much misery within myself, but meditating on the Incarnation of the Son of God, I see with the eyes of my soul the image of a new Man, Who encourages me to impress His features on myself.

---

all possible knowledge that a human mind can contain — indeed, knowledge of all actual things ("relative omniscience" was the classical phrase to describe this; see Jn 16:30 and Col 2:3). Above all, the Divine Son's human soul was infused with the love and mercy of God to an unsurpassable degree.

Chapter 18

MERCY OF GOD, MANIFESTED IN THE WOUNDS OF CHRIST

*"Because with the Lord there is Mercy and
with Him plentiful redemption"*
— Psalm 129 [130]:7

I. The Savior could have made satisfaction for the sins of man with one word, with one prayer to the Father. He could appease Justice through the Incarnation itself, even ransoming man from sin through an act of perfect sorrow. However, such satisfaction would not externally reveal the evil of sin and the infinite power of God's Mercy in its remission. For this reason, He placed in His life so many pains, so much heroism, energy, and power, and especially in His Passion and death did He accept a boundless amount of suffering, the extent of which was manifested through His wounds, remaining [visible] even in His glorified body after the Resurrection. Through His Passion Our Lord wanted to espouse our souls to Himself, and draw them to an ardent love and a tender attachment. He desires to inflame our hearts with the glow of His sufferings, and through the Mercy of His wounds to awaken in us the fire of boundless trust. He wanted likewise to show us the infinite evil of our transgressions, as though He were saying through His wounds to everyone ceaselessly, "Learn from [what sin has done to] Me what sin is."

II. When Jesus was seized in the Garden and painfully bound, wounds might well have appeared. So also the slap on the face He received before Annas, and the beating given while

He was mocked in the prison of Caiaphas, no doubt caused many wounds. However, the greatest, most painful wounds appeared through the scourging, crowning with thorns, and Crucifixion.

The scourging of the Savior was incomparably more severe than that of others condemned to crucifixion, since Pilate, presenting the horrible sight of the scourged Christ, wanted to weaken the hatred of the Jews and turn away their demand for the sentence of death. Furthermore, the more perfect the body, the greater is its sensitivity to pain. The body of Christ, however, was most delicate,[30] and hence it may be assumed that no sufferings could be greater than His; they were even greater than those of all the martyrs. Besides, many [at that time], through the intense pain of scourging, fainted and consequently felt no pain, but Christ, because He sustained Himself by Divine power, was fully conscious during the entire time of His Passion until His final breath on the Cross: "For I am ready for scourges: and my sorrow is continually before me" (Ps 37:18 [38:17]).

The crowning with thorns was a completion of the scourging ordeal. It inflicted pain in the place most sensitive to an exterior stimulus, the head. Without any order from Pilate, the soldiers, for their personal amusement, plaited a crown of piercing thorns and pressed it on His head, driving the thorns into the skin and forcing them through His temples. "And they spat upon Him, and took the reed and kept striking Him on the Head" (Mt 27:30). How great must have been our Savior's pains when the blood blinded His eyes and the blows on His head brought about great dizziness and were a shock to the brain! "We have seen Him, and there was no sightliness, that we should be desirous of Him: despised and the most abject of men, a man of sorrows" (Is 53:2-3).

The crucifixion caused all His wounds to bleed anew. Here Jesus was stripped of His clothes, and new wounds were

---

[30] By "delicate" here Bl. Sopocko does not mean weak or fragile, but perfect in its sensitivity to pleasure and pain, since, according to the classical Catholic Tradition, Christ's humanity was perfect in every way relevant to His mission, as the human nature of God the Son Incarnate.

inflicted on Him. Perhaps the greatest and most poignant of all His wounds was His being nailed to the Cross with blunt nails. Then, the suspension on the Cross gave Him the severest sufferings, which lasted three hours without interruption until His death. Our Savior chose this most painful kind of death [death on a cross] in order that He might make satisfaction to the Divine Justice for our sins and provide for us as ransom the frightful pains on the Cross as evidence of His Mercy.

III. Since the wounds in Jesus' hands, feet, and side were the greatest and most symbolic of His mission, they remained in the glorified body of the Savior even after the Resurrection (Jn 20:27). They are likened to five grains of myrrh that they might be His glory for ever, the evidence of His Mercy on the saints, and the accusation and sentence for the condemned. At the Last Judgment there will gush forth from these wounds a light delighting the chosen and burdening the damned.

Our Lord often proclaimed that He would always remember us. There is nothing that can give us greater assurance of this than the fact that "He inscribed us in His hands" and protects us with His wounds from the punishments of justice.

What the lighthouse is for the sailor so shall these holy wounds be for me. I will seek refuge in them in time of spiritual combat. Here I will learn how to love and make sacrifices. The wounds in His hands will remind me of my duty to labor; the wounds in His feet, of the burdensome roads along which I am to seek souls for Heaven; the wounds of the Heart of Jesus, of His Mercy and my duty to perform acts of mercy.

Chapter 19

MERCY OF GOD, SHOWN IN THE MOST SACRED HEART OF JESUS

"One of the soldiers opened His side with a lance, and immediately there came out Blood and Water"

— John 19:34

I. What a sublime mystery of faith and Mercy is the opening of the side of our Lord. The Fathers of the Church unanimously call the wound in our Savior's side the source of salvation because all the Sacraments, which Christ bequeathed to the Church, flowed from it. As Eve, Adam's spouse, was formed from his side during his sleep, so Holy Mother Church, the Spouse of Jesus Christ, the second Adam, came out from His side when He was asleep with the sleep of death on the cross.

The Evangelist says not that one of the soldiers "pierced" the side of Christ, but that he "opened" it. He opened the gate of life from which innumerable graces of Divine Mercy were to flow continuously, cleansing the souls of sinners through the Sacraments of Baptism and Penance and pouring life into them through the Eucharist and other Sacraments. Though the Evangelist speaks only of the opening of the side, truly the Savior's Heart was also wounded. This fact is established by the Blood and Water, which, as is attested by physicians, gather at the heart of each man immediately after his death. Here also we have a proof that our Lord really died and that afterward He really rose from the dead.

The prophet Joel had already seen in spirit this holy wound of Divine Mercy, for, when prophesying the Lord's judgment over the nation and the glory of the future

Jerusalem, he added these words: "and a fountain shall come forth of the house of the Lord, and shall water the torrent of thorns" (Joel 3:18). The house of the Lord means here Christ's Body, and the sacred wound of His Heart from which the Blood and Water flowed. "The torrent of thorns," according to commentary on Scripture, is the valley of Sitim, where, on their way to the land of Canaan, the Jews lay encamped. This valley was rightly called the "torrent of thorns" because of its lack of water and the infertility of its soil. According to other writers this expression refers to the valley of the Dead Sea, where previously the cities of Sodom and Gomorrah were situated. In both interpretations "the torrent of thorns" symbolized the wretchedness of humanity, which the Divine Mercy, gushing from the opened Heart of Jesus, inundated with graces.

II. Like the fire in the sun, Mercy and compassion are always aflame in the open Heart of Jesus. The sentiments of this Heart are embodied in the behavior of the merciful Samaritan, who does not discriminate according to nationality, descent, dress, or position, but hastens to help one who, in his wretchedness, turns with confidence to him for help. Our Lord gives preference to those who, like the Samaritan, show their love in deeds. "I desire mercy, and not sacrifice" (Mt 9:13); "be merciful" (Lk 6:36) — these are the words of His teaching.

"The thoughts of His Heart to all generations ... to deliver their souls from death and feed them in famine" (Ps 32 [33]:11, and 19). Thus begins the Mass of the Sacred Heart of Jesus. Mercy and compassion are expressed in this verse. It is by His Mercy that God, Who reigned supreme over all creation, drew near to us through His Incarnation and proclaimed that the wretched had a right to live. He Himself comforted the suffering. Then, the Savior bequeathed the precious gift of Mercy to the faithful and, as a result, Christian society became the garden in which Mercy was cultivated. However, before long this garden changed into a field overgrown with cockle. The Lord, however, insists on the old [Christian] tradition, and wherever it comes to life, there the oil of the merciful Samaritan flows again. Today this work is called "social welfare" but it should be renamed "work of mercy" in order that the visible "trademark" of the Merciful Christ be manifest.[31] Then our hearts would be penetrated with the consciousness

---

[31] Blessed Sopocko refers here to the long tradition in the Catholic Church of caring for the poor and the suffering, even through the structural reform of society, when necessary. Historians sometimes claim that after the Constantinian settlement of the fourth century (when Christianity became the official religion of the Roman Empire), the Church compromised itself and no longer cared about the poor and the suffering, much less about the social reform of Europe, except for the protection of its own ecclesiastical properties and privileges. But nothing could be farther from the truth. The historical evidence shows that Bl. Sopocko was entirely right about "the old tradition":

> [I]n the age of Constantine the triumph of Christianity actually brought about a significant transformation of the old Greco-Roman social order. For example, the evils of slavery were mitigated: slave families were kept together, baptized, and married in the Church, and sometimes even ransomed by the Church. In the era of the Fathers it was generally considered a good work before the Lord to free a slave. Christians also elevated the social status of women in the Greco-Roman world. Timothy Keller sums up the evidence for us:

>> It was extremely common in the Greco-Roman world to throw out new female infants to die from exposure, because of the low status of women in society. The church forbade its members to do so. Greco-Roman society saw no value in an unmarried woman, and therefore it was illegal for a widow to go more than two years without remarrying. But Christianity was the first religion to not force widows to marry. They were supported financially and honored within the community so that they were not under great pressure to remarry if they didn't want to. Pagan widows lost all control of their [first] husband's estate when they remarried, but the church allowed widows to maintain their husband's estate. Finally, Christians did not believe in cohabitation. If a Christian man wanted to live with a woman he had to marry her, and this gave women far greater security. Also, the pagan double standard of allowing married men to have extramarital sex and mistresses was forbidden. In all these ways Christian women enjoyed far greater security and equality than did women in the surrounding culture (Timothy Keller, *Walking with God Through Pain and Suffering*. New York: Penguin, 2013, p. 261).

> Indeed, educated women played a key role in Christendom throughout late antiquity and the early Middle Ages: for example, in Byzantium women served both as doctors and as lawyers. In the West, women in the new religious orders ran the schools that often educated the nobility and the future bishops of the Church.

that the Merciful Heart of Jesus will reward us a hundredfold for whatever we do for our fellow human beings. Likewise, we would then be aware that those who help us in any way are showing us His Mercy, and we should feel unworthy of this interweaving of divine and human service, the extension of God's own Mercy.[32]

In this way the Mercy of God springs continually from the Sacred Heart of Jesus, and all of us feel its wonderful and beneficial warmth.

Leaving the altar with the Eucharist, the source of Mercy in my heart, I will follow in the footsteps of the merciful Samaritan to visit the sick, the hungry, the imprisoned, the sorrowful, and the dead.

Some of the most savage aspects of Greco-Roman culture were abolished in the era of Constantine: for example, Christians put an end to the practice of infanticide, and to bloody gladiatorial contests. The laboring classes found relief when Sunday became a day of rest from work for all, and church charities for the poor received imperial financial support. Saint Basil started what may have been the first public hospital, offering free care for the sick; later, Benedictine houses of prayer, study, and hospitality, both to travellers and to the poor, spread across the landscape. Bishop St. Ambrose of Milan forced the Christian Emperor Theodosius to do public penance for an act of mass murder — so even the Emperor was held to be accountable to the laws of God. In short, from the fourth through the ninth centuries, incarnational Christianity did not simply baptise and bless the old pagan imperial culture; rather, it significantly reformed and transformed it. (Robert Stackpole, *The Incarnation.* Chilliwack, BC: The Chartwell Press, first edition, 2019, pp. 553-555).

[32] Blessed Sopocko meant to highlight the fact here that we have not earned or merited the reception of God's merciful love acting through others; it always comes to us as a free gift of God's grace. Thus, by "unworthy" here, he seems to mean simply, "That I do not deserve such a gift" — he does not want to lead us into an unhealthy tendency actually to reject the gifts God gives to us through others out of self-deprecation. His point is that we should be humbled and grateful for the undeserved, but appreciated expressions of God's merciful love, given to us through the human vessels He often uses to bless us with that love.

COMMENTARY:
THE MERCIFUL GOD GIVES US MARY TO BE OUR MOTHER

The one who brings us close to the merciful Heart of Jesus is the Mother of Mercy, the Blessed Virgin Mary. She has this title in God's plan for two reasons, Bl. Sopocko tells us: "she is Mother of Jesus, in Whom Divine Mercy is Incarnate, and she continually shows us mercy" (chapter 20). Her maternal care for us began at the Annunciation, when the angel Gabriel first called her to be the Mother of our Savior, and it continued throughout Her Son's earthly life until she received on Calvary His explicit call to be the Mother of Mercy for us all. Thus she not only conceived and gave birth to Jesus, Divine Mercy Himself; she also, in a sense, conceives and gives birth to our new life in Him. Blessed Sopocko wrote:

> She conceived us at the Annunciation, bore us from the time of the presentation [in the Temple], and brought us forth in pain beneath the cross. "Behold Your son" [Christ's word to her from the Cross] was God's reply to Mary's "fiat" [at the Annunciation]. "You have consented to be My Mother to save sinners; now take them as My brothers. From now on they will be your children and you shall be their Mother, the Mother of Mercy." ... There never was, nor is, nor ever will be a grace given by God in any other way than by Mary's mediation. ... [For] by God's will, no grace is given to us but through the mediation of the Immaculate Heart of Mary (*God is Mercy*, chapters 20 and 21).

For Bl. Michael Sopocko all this was not merely a matter of abstract Mariology; it was a fact of daily life: by her prayers every day Mary takes care of her children as they journey toward the kingdom of her Son. He reasons that if Jesus was born of Mary, and of her consent to be the Mother of the Savior, then all those who are spiritually reborn in Baptism and made members of His Body, the Church, must have been spiritually born of her as well. In other words, we become God's adopted children only by her prayerful consent and supplication. Blessed Sopocko says that by her maternal intercessions she obtains good Christian parents and education for the young, and opportunities for a renewal of faith for those who have fallen away from the faith, and protects her spiritual children from sin throughout our lives. If we should fall into sin despite her prayers, then she prays for our repentance, and that we might return to a state of grace through sacramental Confession. With a true motherly heart, she sorrows over our sins and rejoices when we are reunited with the Mercy of her Son.

In just the two short chapters in this book that he devotes to the Mother of God, Bl. Sopocko shows that what he teaches about her is in full accord with what the Holy Spirit guided the bishops of the Church to write about the Blessed Virgin Mary at the Second Vatican Council:

> The motherhood of Mary, in the order of grace, lasts without interruption from the consent which she faithfully gave at the Annunciation, and which she sustained without hesitation under the Cross, until the eternal fulfillment of all the elect. In fact, being assumed into Heaven, she has not laid aside this office of salvation, but by her manifold intercession, she continues to obtain for us the graces of eternal salvation. By her maternal charity, she takes care of the brethren of her Son, who still journey on earth, surrounded by dangers and difficulties, until they are led into their blessed home (*Lumen Gentium*, 62).

Thus nourished in the depths of our hearts by the Bread of Life, Jesus Himself in the Holy Eucharist, and surrounded by the maternal and loving care of our merciful Mother, we cannot fail to arrive safely at our journey's end, where our Lord and our Lady are waiting to receive us in heavenly glory, and where "eye has not seen, nor the heart of man conceived, the things that God has prepared for those who love Him" (1 Cor 2:9).

Chapter 20

MERCY OF GOD, GIVING TO US THE MOST BLESSED VIRGIN MARY AS MOTHER OF MERCY

"Woman, behold thy son." Then he said to the disciple, "Behold thy mother"
— John 19:26-27

Our Lord dying on the Cross gave us His Mother as Mother of Mercy. Mary is Mother of Mercy under two titles: she is Mother of Jesus, in Whom Divine Mercy is incarnate, and she continually shows us mercy.

I. Of all the titles with which we adorn Mary, the title of the Mother of God is the most magnificent. Here we touch the source and cause of all her sanctity. As the Mother of God she is above all creatures either in Heaven or on earth, and because of her divine maternity she is morally even above any being that God can possibly create. Should it please the Lord to create a new world with new beings more perfect than any creature already in existence, should these beings be far more perfect than the cherubim and seraphim, they would still be lower than Mary, whom the Son of God calls His Mother, and who in return addresses Him as her Son.

As Mother of God she participates in the eternal fecundity of God the Father, Who, before all ages, bears His Son through the comprehension of His own nature.[33]

---

[33] Blessed Sopocko here refers to the traditional Roman Catholic teaching on the Holy Trinity that he explained more fully in chapter 9 (above):

The Father [eternally] recognizes Himself, and through this cognition He gives birth to an Image, living, perfect, and equal to Himself, and

She bears Him in time as God-Man. This is the dignity and greatness at which all Heaven is amazed, and which the wisest cherubim and most perfect seraphim do not fully comprehend. When the eternal Word, being moved by His infinite Mercy, decreed to become flesh, He took this flesh from the most pure womb of Mary. Thus in one Divine Person He united divine nature with human nature and elevated mere human acts to divine worth and dignity.

Mary is the Mother of God in the truest and most exact meaning. All heretics who denied Christ's divinity and the hypostatic union of the two natures in One Divine Person of Jesus — e.g. Nestorius — opposed naming Mary the Mother of God. However, the divine maternity of Mary was defined by the Council of Ephesus (A.D. 431) which based its teaching on the following texts of Scripture: "Behold a virgin shall conceive and bear a son, and his name shall be called Emmanuel" (Is 7:14); "the Holy One to be born shall be called the Son of God" (Lk 1:35). If Mary bore the Son of God, she is the Mother of God. Therefore, Elizabeth, inspired by the Holy Spirit, cried out: "And how have I deserved that the mother of my Lord shall come to me?" (Lk 1:43), thus naming Mary the Mother of God. Saint Paul also says: "God sent his Son, born of a woman" (Gal 4:4). If the One born of a woman is the Son of God, Mary is the Mother of God.

II.   "All the ways of the Lord are mercy and truth" (Ps 24 [25]:10), but Redemption is the greatest work of Divine Mercy. "To have compassion is God's attribute," says St. Hilary, "so above all else we should adore in God His Infinite Mercy, which first of all has been manifested in the Redemption." The work of the Redemption was performed by Jesus Christ, the Son of God, but Mary took an active part in this ineffable mystery. She is truly the Mother of Jesus, Whom she brought forth into the world not merely as a man separated

---

bestows on It His own divine nature. This Image is the Son of God, Who is begotten of the Father, or, in other words, arises from His reason and cognition and is, therefore, called the Wisdom and the Word of God.

from Divinity but as God-Man, our brother and head of the Church, whose members we all are. Truly she brought forth the King of Mercy and is, therefore, Mother of Mercy.

God prepared Mary for the role of Mother of Mercy already through the Immaculate Conception, by which He freed her from original sin from the first moment of her existence. Then at her glorious birth He manifested to the world the attributes bestowed on her by the Divine Mercy: a pure and delicate body, extraordinary qualities of mind, and a strong will, but above all an immaculate and tender Heart. Since the Savior was to be made according to the image and likeness of Mary, it was fitting that Mary be endowed with most sublime natural and supernatural virtues. It is to such a Virgin that the archangel appeared and addressed the words "full of grace," and announced that she would become the Mediatrix of grace, the Mother of the Redeemer, and Mother of Mercy. Mary was fully aware of the great privilege of becoming the Mother of God and, entirely conscious of this, she gave her consent to it. Then she conceived a Son, the King of Mercy, and at the same time spiritually conceived in her womb all His followers.

At the time of the presentation of Jesus in the Temple Mary learned of the dreadful import of the Redemption. She took Jesus from Simeon's arms, but she already knew that the Infant did not belong to her, that He was given to her only as the Lamb Whom she had to feed and rear to be sacrificed and to become the ransom for God's adopted children, for the whole of mankind. What a terrible pain, for which there was no remedy! From this moment Mary, through her care of Jesus, bore us in her heart. She conceived us at the Annunciation, bore us from the time of the Presentation [in the Temple], and brought us forth in pain beneath the cross. "Behold your son" was God's reply to Mary's "fiat" [at the Annunciation]. "You have consented to be My Mother to save sinners; now take them as My brothers. From now on they will be your children and you shall be their Mother, the Mother of Mercy."

The twofold maternity of Mary was a gratuitous grace, bestowed on her without any merits of her own. It was an act of infinite Mercy for her as well as for us.

O Mary, I know that you have not become Mother of Mercy to us all, to me in particular, in vain, but that you will obtain the Mercy of God for me, especially at the hour of my death. From now on I will greet you each morning and evening with ever-increasing fervor.

Chapter 21

MARY
CONTINUALLY BESTOWS
MERCY UPON US

"Whatsoe'er may be
Of excellence in creature, pity mild,
Relenting mercy, large munificence,
Are all combined in thee."

— Dante, *Paradiso*, canto xxxiii, 19-21

I. Mary beneath the Cross immediately assumed, as it were, the office of Mother of Mercy and began to bestow mercy on sinners. She beheld the dying thief hanging on the Cross beside Jesus and decided to adopt him as her son and thus became Mother of Mercy to him. Looking up at him with sorrowful eyes she encouraged him to trust and to speak to Jesus. At the same time, she implored the Savior to show Mercy to the thief. Thanks to this intercession Dismas was so completely converted that he at once spoke in defense of his insulted Lord, publicly confessed his faults, repented for them, begged pardon and lived to hear that most consoling assurance: "This day thou shalt be with Me in paradise" (Lk 23:43).[34]

---

[34] Our Lady's role in the conversion of the Good Thief on Calvary is not mentioned in Holy Scripture, but comes from later tradition, based (it would seem) on the reasonable supposition that as she stood and prayed beneath the Cross, she must have prayed also for the salvation of the two men crucified alongside her Son, and encouraged them to have faith in Him.

From this time on[35] Mary became Mediatrix of all graces and the actual Mother of Mercy to all people. There never was, nor is, nor ever will be a grace given by God in any other way than by Mary's mediation. She obtained the grace of fortitude for St. Stephen, the first martyr of faith in Christ. She strengthened the apostles in time of persecution and fortified them in their toils and labors. She obtained the conversion of Saul and helped St. Paul in his apostolic labors among the pagans. She was the inspiration of the Evangelists, the fortitude of the martyrs, the purity of the virgins, the perseverance of the confessors, the light of the Doctors of the Church. For the Holy Spirit poured His graces of Mercy on all men solely through her Immaculate Heart.[36] After she was assumed into Heaven Mary did not cease to take care of the world and to obtain Divine Mercy for her adopted children.

Jesus is the Head of the Mystical Body of which we became members through Baptism. If Jesus was born of Mary, all those who are part of Jesus must also be born spiritually of her. We became God's adopted children only through Mary's consent, for her motherly Heart desired and willed it and prayed for it. While so many millions of people lack the faith, she obtained it for us. By her entreaties she won for us Christian parents, true education, and protection, and with a mother's care she noticed the reactions of our will to the devil's suggestions. Perhaps we can remember more than a few

---

[35] Of course, Catholic Tradition generally holds that she was Mediatrix of Mercy also because she received into her womb and into the world the merciful Savior. Blessed Sopocko probably meant here from the moment Jesus entrusted her to His Beloved Disciple — "Son, behold your mother" (Jn 19:25-27). In that sense, the conversion of the Good Thief may have been the first actual instance of her role as intercessory, maternal Mediatrix of Mercy for the conversion of sinners on the basis of the Passion of her Son.

[36] Blessed Sopocko may be referring here to the theological tradition which holds that through God's eternal vision of the Incarnation, Passion, and death of His eternal Son, He poured out His graces upon human beings of all times and places in human history. Insofar as the Heart of Mary was the special vessel of the Incarnation in time, and spiritually united with her Son in a special way when He was dying on the Cross, in that sense it may be held that all graces of the Holy Spirit received by all human beings in every age pass through her Immaculate Heart. Saint Bernard of Clairvaux (1090-1153), for example, was fond of calling Our Lady the "aqueduct" of all divine grace (*Sermon for the Nativity of the Blessed Virgin Mary*, 6).

sins in the span of our life — Mary wept because of them. She considered the best means of correction, like reproaches of conscience, adversities, or failures — all this to compel us to enter into ourselves. Perhaps we have been spiritually dead in mortal sin? With what solicitude did Mary then obtain for us the grace of resurrection to the life of grace through the Sacrament of Penance! Let it remain a secret known to God alone how many times we have caught ourselves in the same snare; the more frequently it happened, the more we obtained the special sorrow and loving attention of the Mother of Mercy.

II. What motherly solicitude! When we recall its working in our life, we can only wonder at her power and clearness of vision. It was she who, so many times, moved her Son to pardon us like the thief on the cross. She saved many of us from eternal punishment which sin deserved. We shall learn in Heaven the number of sinners snatched from the hands of Justice by Mary's intercession. We will know only in eternity whether a punishment that had already been decreed against us was stayed by the tender hand of the Mother of Mercy.

The moment of conversion is not the same for all. Saint Augustine, St. Mary of Egypt, and many others spent a considerable part of their lives far from God, while others were ravished by grace from the very beginning. But however we may be converted, the Mother of Mercy is always the instrumental cause, for, by God's will, no grace is given to us but through the mediation of the Immaculate Heart of Mary. Let us not be too certain that we are safe now and have no need of our Mother's care. Like little children we should always remain under her mantle, to press continually to the bosom of our Mother who nurses and rears us and obtains mercy for us. Indeed, all grace comes from the most Merciful Jesus, but without Mary's prayer and adoption no grace is poured on us.[37]

---

[37] Blessed Sopocko seems to be referring here to Our Lady's state in Heaven now. A Catholic theological tradition holds that, while in Heaven the saints are not omniscient, they do see in the Beatific Vision all that they need to see that pertains to their own role in the Kingdom of God. Thus, if Mary's role now is to be the Mother and Mediatrix of Mercy for all, she probably does not need to know molecular physics,

God rules the world and distributes His Mercy through secondary causes, the principal one of which is the Mother of Mercy. The numerous miraculous shrines where, before an image or statue of Mary, people receive many temporal and spiritual graces, are the best proof of it.

> *Having no power to support itself a young ivy leans on other plants and climbs up them. My soul, lean on the Mother of Mercy; and like her, you will climb the height. Then you will have a sweet solace in knowing that it was Mary who has lifted you up. The weaker and poorer we are, the more let us press to the bosom of Our Mother like infants. Let us repeat with tender childlike trust and we shall never be disappointed, "O Mother of Mercy, we fly to Thy patronage, O Holy Mother of God."*

---

the speed travelled by each of the galaxies, or the details of biological evolution, but she would need to see by a gift of God the movements of each human heart for whose conversion and growth in grace she continually prays.

Chapter 22

MERCY OF GOD, MANIFESTED IN THE INSTITUTION OF THE UNIVERSAL CHURCH

"Christ loved the Church, and delivered Himself up for her"
— Ephesians 5:25

I. Christ came to earth not only for those who were living in the Holy Land during His time but for all people always. Therefore, after He had taken away His visible presence from us He left us, as it were, another self: the Church, which He entrusted with His teaching, power, worship, and Sacraments. We find Christ in the Church. Moreover, no one comes to Christ other than through the Church. "No one comes to the Father but through Me" (Jn 14:6). We do not belong to Christ unless we belong to the Church actually or by desire (as do the catechumens).[38] Nor do we live the life of Christ except through communion with the Church.

The Church is a visible society. First of all, it is visible in its hierarchy, composed of the Vicar of Christ, the successor of Peter, and of the bishops and priests remaining in communion with him. The hierarchy teaches, rules and sanctifies in the name of Christ. From the time of the Incarnation, God, in His relation to us, has acted through men in whom Christ's

---

[38] According to Catholic teaching, this desire for unity with Christ in His Body, the Church, can be *explicit,* as it is with catechumens as they prepare for adult Baptism; or *implicit,* as it is for all those who are sincerely seeking the truth, but who lived before, or outside the reach of effective Catholic evangelism, or who had the Catholic faith poorly presented to them in some way. Such persons are in a state of what the Church calls "invincible ignorance" of the truth of the Catholic faith, in other words, a lack of belief that is not primarily their own fault. See *Catechism,* 847.

power remained, "He who hears you, hears Me" (Lk 10:16). The Church is also visible in its ordinary members, in those who are incorporated by Baptism into the Mystical Body of Christ (Eph 2:19-22) and have not severed themselves from it by either heresy or schism. We call the Church a Mystical Body not only to distinguish it from Christ's physical body but also to stress the truth that the union of Christ with the Church is supernatural, that is, based on mysteries accessible by faith alone, and that it draws its life from these mysteries. The Church is a living organism having its life through the Holy Spirit with the grace of Christ.

Christ cannot be fully comprehended without the Church, and vice versa: the Church cannot be understood in abstraction from Christ. The Church is united to Him as inseparably as the body is united to the head. To strike the Church, that is to say, the persons who by Baptism and a life of grace are Christ's members, means to strike Christ Himself. "Saul, Saul, why dost thou persecute Me? (Acts 9:4), said Christ to Saul, who was busy persecuting the Christians. We are all one with Christ. We all live the same life of grace under one Head, and directed by one Spirit we remain mutually united to each other, to the blessed in Heaven and to the Holy Souls suffering in Purgatory, "That all may be one" (Jn 17:21).

II. Just as Christ embodies the infinite Mercy of God in His Person, so the Church, His Spouse, makes this Mercy effective for all time. First of all, the Son of God through infinite Mercy united Himself hypostatically to human nature, and now He seeks to unite Himself to the whole of human society, which He desires to change into His Mystical Body.[39]

---

[39] That is, Christ seeks to do so primarily through the spread of the Gospel, conversion, and Baptism, so that ultimately all of humanity may be incorporated into His Body, the Church (see Mt 28:18-20; Eph 1:10; Col 1:20). Blessed Sopocko actually expressed this more emphatically, according to the original English translation ("He unites Himself to the whole of human society, which He changes into His Mystical Body"), but that phrasing might mislead readers today into thinking that he was an adherent of the doctrine of universal salvation, so we have revised his text slightly here to bring out what was evidently his intended meaning.

The satisfaction and merits of Christ have become our own, for God, placated by the Head, forgets the offenses committed by the members provided they are closely united to the Head through grace.[40] The Incarnate Word finds in the Church [that portion of humanity] which partakes of God's friendship through Him: "The Father Himself loves you, because you have loved Me, and have believed that I came forth from God" (Jn 16:27). Like the Merciful Savior the Church, His Spouse, following in the footsteps of the compassionate Samaritan, pours the wine of contrition and the oil of confidence into the wounds of her children, and entreats individuals, societies, and nations to return to communion with Christ that she may direct them to our common heavenly home. When we read the Acts of the Apostles, we see how God miraculously extended His Church, and maintained and directed it for the good of humanity and of particular nations and individuals. When we study the history of the Church, we learn how the Church made Divine Mercy real for all nations and all ages, and how its influence reached even to those nations that were yet unaware of the Mercy of God or had fallen away from it.

What do a confessional, a baptismal font, a pulpit, a Communion rail suggest to us? All of them speak to us about the infinite Mercy of God. At the baptismal font, Divine Mercy makes us God's children; from the pulpit, it teaches us; in the confessional, it absolves us of our sins. Is it possible that we should not exclaim with the prophet, "If I forget thee, O Jerusalem (the Church of Christ), let my right hand be forgotten. Let my tongue cleave to my jaws, if I do not remember thee" (Ps 136 [137]:5-6)?

I owe love, respect, and obedience to the Church, for she is my Mother; she is the Merciful Jesus Himself.

---

[40] Blessed Sopocko does not mean literally that God "forgets" our offenses, since God is always omniscient. "Forgets" here is just a metaphorical expression referring to the fact that God forgives and pardons our offenses, so that we can put the past behind us, so to speak. Blessed Sopocko is simply using a way of speaking of God's forgiveness that is often found in Holy Scripture (e.g. Ps 25:7; Is 43:25).

COMMENTARY:
THE MERCIFUL GOD REFRESHES
US IN THE SACRAMENTS

Take any long hike through the hills and valleys of the countryside, and you will need refreshment along the way, or you will not make it to the end of your journey. Along the road to Heaven, our Merciful Savior has provided us with fountains of refreshment, grace, and peace in the Sacraments of His Church. Blessed Michael Sopocko writes:

> Just as Christ embodies the infinite Mercy of God in His Person, so the Church, His Spouse, makes this Mercy effective for all time. ... What do a confessional, a baptismal font ... a Communion rail suggest to us? All of them speak to us about the infinite Mercy of God. At the baptismal font, Divine Mercy makes us God's children; ... in the confessional, it absolves us of our sins; ... it is God's mercy that makes [all of] them instruments of grace. ... The Holy Sacraments are ... instruments through which Divine Mercy pours streams of grace on the Church, the whole of the world, and all people in all ages. ... Indeed, the Sacraments continually renew the face of the earth (*God is Mercy*, chapters 22 and 23).

These special, sacramental graces first flow into our hearts at our Baptism where we are adopted into God's family, and we begin to swim for the first time in the ocean of His infinite mercy. If you have never thought of yourself as a "fish for the Lord," then read this passage from *God is Mercy*:

> What great graces of Divine Mercy flow into the soul during Holy Baptism, by which we become

members of the Mystical Body of Christ and the living temple of the Holy Spirit! The most common symbol of the early Christians was the fish, which can survive only in water. Water is also the life-giving element and the matter of Baptism. "We are fishes of Christ; we are born in water and only in it we remain alive" (Tertullian, *De Baptis*, 6,1) (*God is Mercy*, chapter 24).

A soul who refuses to cooperate with baptismal grace, however, is like a fish that tries to live on its own on land — a "fish out of water," so to speak. Before long it is wriggling in the sand and gasping for breath. To rescue us from this disaster, our Lord has provided us with a sacramental remedy:

> The sickness of the soul is ... more painful and more serious than the illness of the body, and the reproaches of conscience often greatly exceed physical suffering. They undermine the health of the body; weaken the strength, firmness, and fortitude of the soul; destroy its peace and hamper its flight to God. Furthermore, they make the soul morose and enclosed within itself, irritable, and ill-disposed to others. They deprive it of eagerness to pray, desire to work, and readiness to carry on the spiritual struggle, and sometimes even incite the soul to new transgressions.
>
> Our Lord gave us, for this kind of disease of the soul, a wonderful remedy in the Sacrament of Penance. "Go in peace and sin no more" are the words spoken to the penitent by Christ's representative. Our hearts melt at the very memory of this, tears come to our eyes, and a blissful feeling penetrates our souls. Truly this Sacrament is the fount of cures for the sick and suffering. Even physicians witness the improvement of health in the sick who have made a good confession. ...

How many broken down and hopeless hearts has our Lord raised up and soothed by this Sacrament! ... Truly, there is in it the superabundance of Divine Mercy (*God is Mercy*, chapters 32 and 25).

Notice that all this is very similar to what Jesus taught St. Faustina, about this same Sacrament:

Daughter, when you go to confession, the fountain of My mercy, the Blood and Water which came forth from My Heart, always flows down upon your soul, and ennobles it. Every time you go to confession, immerse yourself entirely in My mercy, with great trust, so that I may pour the bounty of My grace upon your soul. When you approach the confessional know this, that I myself am waiting there for you. I am only hidden by the priest, but I myself act in your soul. Here the misery of the soul meets the God of mercy. Tell souls that from this fount of mercy souls draw graces solely with the vessel of trust. If their trust is great, there is no limit to My generosity. The torrents of grace inundate humble souls (*Diary*, 1602).

Another critical moment on the life journey of the soul is the moment of death itself.[41] Here everything in the spiritual life either comes to completion or crashes in flames. Blessed Sopocko teaches that, since our eternal life depends on our perseverance in faith, hope, and love, Satan usually assaults the souls of the dying with great ferocity, inciting them to lose their trust in God. He tries to drive away from our hearts any sense that we are still children of God, our Merciful Father. As a result, it often happens that people who are gravely ill find it difficult to pray, are impatient with their sufferings, and are irritable with those who care for them. If

---

[41] See note 65, below, on the nature and use of the Sacrament of Anointing (Extreme Unction].

possible, the devil will even drive the soul to despair of God's love altogether. Once again, however, our Merciful Savior has provided a sacramental remedy for us:

> The Merciful Christ has prepared a special help for this most important and dreadful moment of a person's whole life, that is, the Sacrament of Extreme Unction [i.e., Anointing of the Sick]. It imparts special graces to the dying man, and takes away his sins, evil inclinations, and the like. This Sacrament uplifts the spirit and confirms it in good, and it even has the power to restore bodily health. ...
>
> Above all else, Extreme Unction uplifts the spirit of the dying person ... awakening great trust in the Mercy of God so that the sick individual suffers with patience all the inconveniences and pains that trouble him, and resists the temptations of Satan with greater fortitude. ... So we may assert that Extreme Unction is one of the greatest works of the Mercy of God (*God is Mercy*, chapter 37).

In this way, by sacramental means of grace, the Merciful Jesus refreshes us both at the beginning and at the end of our life journey (that is, by Baptism, and by the Anointing of the Sick), and He comes to our rescue through the Sacrament of Reconciliation whenever we fall into sin. But a life pathway has more than just a beginning, an end, and moments of spiritual crisis along the way. Without daily bread to strengthen us for the journey, we could never climb the hills and find our way through the valleys along our path. It is for this reason that our Savior gave us the most important Sacrament of all: the Sacrament of the Bread of Life (Jn 6:35-59). See later in this book the Commentary: "The Merciful God Gives Himself to Us in the Blessed Sacrament."

Chapter 23

MERCY OF GOD, CONTAINED IN THE INSTITUTION OF THE HOLY SACRAMENTS

"Unless a man be born again of water and the Spirit, he cannot enter into the kingdom of God"

— John 3:5

I. The Holy Sacraments are visible signs of divine grace. As the visible signs, composed of matter and form, they are simple elements, without life; it is God's Mercy that makes them the instruments of grace. All the graces of the Sacraments have one main goal: our likeness to Christ, imparting to us His supernatural life, our gradual transformation into Him. Since sanctifying grace is the basis of supernatural life, the main work of the Sacraments consists in supplying us with it. Another effect of some Sacraments is [the gift of] a character through which the soul participates in the triple dignity of Christ: as a citizen of the Kingdom of God (Baptism), as a knight in this Kingdom (Confirmation), as a priest of Christ (Holy Orders). The third result of the Sacraments is a communication or increase of all the supernatural virtues and gifts, which flow from sanctifying grace as from their source. The fourth effect is the gift of special auxiliary graces, which we need in various situations of our state of life. Finally, the fifth result is the indwelling in the soul of the Holy Spirit Himself, the Author of all supernatural gifts.

The efficacy of the Sacraments rests on some immutable laws, on the divine action independent of the person who administers the Sacraments, and even of him who receives them. Strictly speaking, the person receiving the Sacraments is obliged only to put no obstacles in the way to obstruct their work in him. On our side, there is no cause of the operation of grace, but only a preparation and a condition for obtaining it.[42] God Himself operates in the Sacraments, and this is all that is needed. Consequently, the Sacraments produce grace by Divine Power and efficacious force. In God's plan, they are the true causes of grace. They are powerful instruments with which God acts to produce grace in our hearts. For the Sacraments are operations effected in Christ's name, and thanks to His decree and order, by virtue of His infinite merits, they infallibly induce God to grant grace. They produce this result by Divine Power and reach beyond all natural causes.

II. The Sacraments are the work of the special Mercy of God, for through them the operation of grace is effected completely, instantly, with inexhaustible abundance, and with compassionate application to all conditions of humanity in all times and in all spiritual circumstances. In some cases, one Sacrament replaces another and produces its effects. For instance, according to a well-established opinion, the Eucharist can, to a certain degree, bring about the effects of the Sacrament of Penance. Extreme Unction completes all other Sacraments with respect to taking away actual sins;[43] moreover, like the Sacrament of Penance, it restores those merits that the soul had acquired before it fell from grace by sin. In other words, that which sin broke down and destroyed

---

[42] Here Bl. Sopocko refers to the fact that in order to receive the grace signified by a Sacrament, we need only make sure that we have placed no obstacles in the way of that inflow of grace (for example, by unrepented sin, or by a refusal to believe in the grace of the Sacrament itself). In order for that sacramental grace to bear fruit in our lives in an increase of virtue, and in works of authentic faith and love, however, Bl. Sopocko taught (along with the Catholic Tradition generally) that we must actively prepare our hearts with the right dispositions to receive the Sacraments (for example, preparing for Holy Communion by fostering in ourselves deep trust in God's merciful love, and faith in the Real Presence of Jesus in the consecrated Host), and then we must cooperate with the sacramental graces we have received (see, for example, Bl. Sopocko's discussion of cooperation with grace in chapters 4, 5, and 30 in this book).

[43] By "completes" here Bl. Sopocko refers to the fact that typically this Sacrament is received at the end of one's life, completing one's sacramental journey to the Lord.

is raised again by the vivifying power of the Sacraments. The Holy Sacraments are the laws established by God to endure, and to be instruments through which Divine Mercy pours streams of grace on the Church, the whole of the world, and all people in all ages.[44] By virtue and authority of this Mercy the faithful, through Baptism, become heirs of the Kingdom of God. Sinners obtain forgiveness of their faults in the Sacraments of Penance and Extreme Unction. They become Christ's soldiers in Confirmation. Chosen souls partake in the very priesthood of Christ by consecrating and receiving His true Body. Who can comprehend how deeply the work of the Sacraments penetrates the Church and the entire world? How many crimes are stamped out by them, how many punishments are averted from humanity, how many joys do they cause, how many sufferings do they calm and soothe? Indeed, the Sacraments continually renew the face of the earth; change this valley of tears into a paradise; and fill the Church with graces, making it God's garden, all green and full of flowers and ripening fruit.

Let us revere the Sacraments, which are so sublime, so infallible, so strong, so various in their operation, so inexhaustible in their effects. These sources of grace will never dry up, even though we cease to receive them or begin to abuse them. They are our consolation in life and after death. Let us thank the Merciful Christ for them and be wise in profiting by them.

---

[44] The Sacraments might be seen as "laws" in the sense that if they are celebrated and administered with the proper form, matter and intention, as given to us by our Lord through His Church, then without fail they will convey the grace they signify, just as if you do what is required by the laws of physics to produce water (that is, combine hydrogen and oxygen in the proper proportions), then by the laws of nature, without fail you will get water (see *Catechism*, 1127-1128).

Chapter 24

MERCY OF GOD, BESTOWED UPON HUMANITY IN THE SACRAMENT OF BAPTISM

*"According to His mercy, He saved us,
through the bath of regeneration,
and renewal by the Holy Spirit"*

— Titus 3:5

I. Since human beings are composed of soul and body, God gives us spiritual graces in sensible signs, so that through material and visible things we might more easily arrive at a knowledge of those which are spiritual and invisible. Therefore, justification or interior regeneration is made dependent on two causes: water and the Holy Spirit. The Holy Spirit is the effective cause of the grace, and the water [of Baptism] is the instrumental cause.

By bodily birth man is merely a natural being, dead to the supernatural life. The original sin with which he comes into the world is not only a lack of the supernatural life, but a real sin of nature. It constitutes in us a state of alienation from God and of slavery to Satan. Baptism removes sin, releases us from Satan's dominion, and grants us a higher nature endowed with the capacities for supernatural life, which it effects through sanctifying grace. "Repent and be baptized every one of you in the name of Jesus Christ for the forgiveness of your sins; and you will receive the gift of the Holy Spirit" (Acts 2:38).

Baptism not only takes away sins but also remits the punishment due to them, for it incorporates us into the Passion and death of our Savior and assigns His merits to us. "We were buried with Him by means of baptism into death" (Rom 6:4). The afflictions of this life are not removed by Baptism, for by them Christians become more like Christ and receive an opportunity of acquiring merits. These afflictions do not have the character of a penalty, but are properties of our infirm nature.

Moreover, Baptism procures the sacramental grace of regeneration, which means that along with sanctifying grace it gives us a right to special actual graces which consist in enlightenment in the truths of faith, so that we can better understand and live by them, and behave according to them. Whence Baptism is also named the Sacrament of Faith.

Finally, Baptism impresses a sacramental character on the soul like an indelible seal or like a sign burned on the arm with an iron. This sign always inheres in the soul. The devils, as the Fathers say, shudder and flee from it. "Now it is God ... Who has anointed us, Who has also stamped us with his seal" (2 Cor 1:21-21).

II. What great graces of Divine Mercy flow into the soul during Holy Baptism, by which we become members of the Mystical Body of Christ and the living temple of the Holy Spirit! The most common symbol of the early Christians was the fish, which can survive only in water. Water is also the life-giving element and the matter of Baptism. "We are the fishes of Christ; we are born in water and only in it we remain alive" (Tertullian, *De baptis.* 6, 1).

Water is considered the pure vivifying element on earth. Without it, all is dead. Happily, it is found almost everywhere. For this reason, Christ chose it for the matter of the first and most necessary Sacrament, in which the pouring of water together with the pronouncing of the sacramental words is followed by the interior cleansing of the soul and its regeneration to new life. The ceremonies that precede Baptism are the following: solemn exorcism; renunciation of all Satan's works; breathing on the face of the child; anointing of the ears, nostrils, breast, and shoulders with oil, and lastly, the placing of a bit of salt in the mouth of the baptized.[45] All this symbolizes the arousing and preparing of all our faculties for the super-natural acts of understanding, of accepting and professing the truths of faith, of vigorous and firm combat against Satan, and of perseverance in fulfilling the commandments of God and of the Church. Even the giving of a name to the baptized and the presence of the godfather and godmother mean that a new life, a new birth to God and the Church, begins here. In Baptism a child is born not according to the laws of nature but, by the infinite Mercy of God, as becomes God's child, one of those "who were born of God" (Jn 1:13).

It would be fitting to ring the bells of the church on the day of Baptism and to celebrate the anniversary of this event with great joy and gratitude. It would be becoming to set aside the vestment received for this solemnity and the candle, so that they might always remind us of the duties of a Christian. Saint Louis, the king of France, used to sign his name as "Louis of Poissy," for the place of his Baptism was dearer to him than the whole of France.

I obtained supernatural life through Baptism that I might live, think, speak, and act supernaturally. I will often thank God for this grace and remember the moment of my Baptism with joy, turning with trust to the Merciful Christ with Whom I clothed myself, so that I may respond to my vocation as a Christian.

---

[45] Blessed Sopocko is referring here to the baptismal rite of the Catholic Church prior to the Second Vatican Council; he mentions some but not all of the ceremonies that precede Baptism in the Old Rite. Some aspects of that rite were simplified after the Council, while the basic structure of the rite remains the same. Today, in churches of the Roman rite, the basic ceremonies preceding the Baptism itself are: (1) the priest traces the Sign of the Cross on the forehead of the candidate; (2) a prayer is said for exorcism, and a renunciation of all Satan's works; and (3) the priest anoints the candidate with the Oil of Catechumens, blessed by the bishop. Breathing on the candidate's face and the placing of salt in the candidate's mouth, however, are no longer parts of the official rite.

Chapter 25

MERCY OF GOD, BESTOWED UPON HUMANITY IN THE SACRAMENT OF PENANCE

"God is compassionate and merciful,
and will forgive sins"
— Sirach 2:13

I. The memory of sins committed and the reproaches of conscience that accompany this memory are the greatest misfortunes for us, since nothing and no one can free us from them. No science, art, or culture, nor any power in the world, is of any avail in this respect; God alone can forgive sin. The heart feels this instinctively. Should anyone desire to liberate himself from sin in any other way, he would deceive himself, for he would not understand the things of God. "Thy sins are forgiven" (Lk 7:48), said our Lord to Mary Magdalen. He also said to the contrite paralytic, "Man, thy sins are forgiven thee" (Lk 5:20). The ineffable and benign Mercy of the God-Man sounds in these words. The Savior handed down the power of forgiving sins to the apostles in the cenacle, when He breathed on them and said, "Whose sins you shall forgive, they are forgiven them; and whose sins you shall retain, they are retained" (Jn 20:23). The priest, therefore, has the power of forgiving and retaining sins, which power he exercises according to the state of the soul of the penitent. The sinner has to repent of his faults, accuse himself of having committed them, and make satisfaction for them.[46] Sorrow, confession of sins, and satisfaction are necessary acts; they

---

[46] That is, to perform the required penance assigned to us in sacramental Confession, with the proper dispositions of faith, hope, and love.

119

constitute, as it were, the matter of the Sacrament of Penance, while the words of absolution are its form.[47] In this way the sinner obtains forgiveness of all his sins, be they grave or light, and pardon of the eternal punishment and, in part, of the temporal.[48] His former merits are restored and he is given a special sacramental grace, which secures for him the right to actual graces to uproot the remains of sins, such as evil inclinations, and bad customs and habits. It is the real, interior justification that transforms and makes a new creature of the sinner, and renews his soul before God. From being a sinner he becomes God's child, a new, transformed being, a pure and holy creature.

II. Along with Baptism, the Sacrament of Penance is the greatest manifestation of the Mercy of God. This Sacrament is rightly called "Baptism by toil" or "the second plank after shipwreck." When the ship of baptismal innocence, which was to carry us to the country of eternal happiness, has been wrecked, the Merciful Jesus compassionately offers us the "plank" of Penance. In order to save himself the wretched man has to catch hold of it, to cling to it with both hands despite all difficulties, amid bitter waves of contrition, confession of sins, and satisfaction.

In this easy way our sins are taken away and we recover all that we had lost. We regain lost rights and the respect of the Church, a recovery that in ancient times was marked by a special ceremony when public penance was finished. God also looks kindly on penitents because they recover their innocence and supernatural merits. Nay, rather, they become even richer than before their fall, since they obtain an assurance of peace [with God].

---

[47] Here, as elsewhere in this book, Bl. Sopocko uses terms derived from Aristotle: "form" and "matter." The matter of a Sacrament is the external, sacramental sign used (for example, water in Baptism; oil in the sacramental Anointing of the Sick). The "form" is the intention and meaning of that sign, as expressed in the Liturgy (for example, in Baptism, the pouring of water in the name of the Trinity to impart the grace of regeneration; in the Anointing of the Sick, the application of oil accompanied by prayer for physical and spiritual healing).

[48] For the distinction between the temporal and eternal punishment of sin, see *Catechism*, 1472-1473.

How many broken down and hopeless hearts has our Lord raised up and soothed by this Sacrament! How many families, how many parishes have found peace and harmony through it! It is an inexhaustible treasure for societies, states, and nations. It would be such a treasury for the whole world, if only everybody would receive it worthily. Truly, there is in it the superabundance of Divine Mercy. "Seek ye the Lord, while He may be found: call upon Him while He is near" (Is 55:6). In this Sacrament I come in contact with the Savior. His Blood pours on me and cleans me of guilt.

O Merciful Jesus, I thank You for this Sacrament of Mercy! I will approach Your tribunal with sorrow and confidence, and on leaving the confessional I will make a heartfelt act of thanksgiving. I will, with the greatest devotion, consider the mercies of the Lord toward all of humanity on Low Sunday [that is, the Sunday after Easter, now called "Divine Mercy Sunday], because that is the octave day of the solemn Baptism administered to the catechumens [on Easter Sunday] (hence the Latin name [of the Sunday after Easter], Dominica in Albis [literally, the "Sunday in White"] referring to the white garments worn by the catechumens from Good Friday to Low Sunday [according to the custom of the early Church] as a sign that their sins had been washed away); and because it is also the octave of the institution of the Sacrament of Penance and indulgences, and consequently the octave of the completion of the Sacrament of Holy Orders from which Sacraments the Mercy of God continuously pours out upon mankind.

COMMENTARY:
THE MERCIFUL GOD GIVES HIMSELF TO US IN THE BLESSED SACRAMENT

We have been meditating with Bl. Sopocko on the blessings and graces that our Lord provides to aid us on our journey to the heavenly kingdom. Now we come to His greatest gift of all: the Holy Eucharist.

Blessed Sopocko wrote that the Eucharist "is a masterpiece of the love of Our Lord," for in it He unites us in the very depths of our hearts with His infinite Mercy:

> The Eucharist ... reveals the love of Jesus for each of the members of the Church, for He gives Himself to each of them. Desiring to be the source of Divine Life in them, Jesus takes on the form of nourishment to come close to us and penetrate into the recesses of our hearts, where He exalts, consoles, and enriches us, and gives Himself to us as a pledge of future happiness (*God is Mercy*, chapter 26).

The Eucharist is a stupendous miracle, Fr. Sopocko says: the transformation of the bread and wine into the Body and Blood, Soul and Divinity of Jesus Christ. Although God is present everywhere in the universe through His Divine Power and Wisdom, in the Blessed Sacrament Jesus fulfills His promise to His disciples to remain always with us (Mt 28:20), for He makes not only His divinity, but also His risen and glorified humanity, uniquely present to us in the consecrated Host. Blessed Sopocko writes:

> God is, in a more particular manner, present in our sanctuaries, called the house of prayer in the Scriptures. Here God is, as it were, sitting on the throne of Mercy so that He might graciously hear

the prayers of suppliants. Here Jesus veils His divine as well as His human brilliance so that we might approach Him as did the Samaritan woman and draw from the spring of life, which is His Heart. Here really and truly "God is with us" (*God is Mercy*, chapter 35).

The Eucharist is also the source of all the divine graces that we receive in our lives. Blessed Sopocko calls it a "miraculous multiplication of the angelic bread," which pours out graces on zealous and lukewarm souls alike (chapter 41). For this reason, he loved to enumerate all the blessings and benefits we receive from devout reception of our Lord in this Sacrament. For him, the "effects of the Eucharist are the most clear proof that the infinite mercy of God is there present." He wrote:

> As bodily food serves to build the physical side of human beings, so the Blessed Sacrament revives and heals, protects and strengthens, feeds and develops the supernatural life of the soul. Here is effected the closest union with Christ, not only a spiritual but also a physical union with such tangibility and perfection that no closer union on earth is possible. Moreover, this Sacrament ... imparts to us a special grace of devotion and of ardent love from which come happiness and bliss, peace and fortitude, and boundless readiness for sacrifices for God and our neighbor (*God is Mercy*, chapter 26).

On the centrality and importance of the Holy Eucharist, Bl. Sopocko and St. Faustina were obviously kindred spirits. Many of the most ardent and passionate sections of St. Faustina's *Diary* concern her love for Jesus in the Eucharist, and her amazement at the extraordinary graces He poured out on her soul through this Sacrament:

> All the good that is in me is due to Holy Communion. ... Herein lies the whole secret of my sanctity.

... One thing alone sustains me, and that is Holy Communion. From it I draw all my strength; in it is all my comfort. ... Jesus concealed in the Host is everything to me. ... I would not know how to give glory to God if I did not have the Eucharist in my heart. ... O living Host, my one and only strength, fountain of love and mercy, embrace the whole world, and fortify faint souls. O blessed be the instant and the moment when Jesus left us His most merciful Heart! (*Diary*, 1392, 1489, 1037, and 223)

Father Sopocko was inspired, above all, by the divine motive clearly manifest in the gift to us of the Blessed Sacrament: "for the Lord works with such freedom and gratuity ... only by reason of His boundless compassion for human wretchedness" (chapter 26). Here God's Mercy is on full display. Do not be deceived, therefore, by the fact that Bl. Sopocko devotes only one short chapter in this book to the wonder and miracle of the Mass. That chapter is full of superlatives. After all, when you have reached the top of the mountain, there is not much more to say. As Bl. Sopocko puts it: "The incomparable beauty of the Catholic Church is a flower and fruit of the mystery of the Holy Eucharist."

Chapter 26

MERCY OF GOD, GRANTED IN THE SACRAMENT OF THE ALTAR

"He who eats my flesh ...
he also shall live because of Me"
— John 6:57-58

I. The Eucharist is above all else a Sacrament of love. Here is revealed the love of God for Himself, which consists in glorifying Himself through the manifestation of His Wisdom, Power, Goodness, and Mercy, and through moving men to give Him glory by their adoration and homage.[49]

The Eucharist also reveals the love of Jesus for each of the members of the Church, for He gives Himself to each of them. Desiring to be the source of Divine Life in them, Jesus takes on the form of nourishment to come close to us and penetrate into the recesses of our hearts, where He exalts, consoles, and enriches us, and gives Himself to us as a pledge of future happiness.

---

[49] Blessed Sopocko may be referring here to the prayer of Christ in St. John's Gospel, chapter 17, the night of the institution of the Holy Eucharist. In this prayer, He asks the Father that His "glory" (that is, His eternal divine glory, especially the eternal love between the Father and the Son) may shine out in His Passion, death, and Resurrection, for the Son gave His life not only for the salvation of sinners, but also to return the lost world back to the love and embrace of His Heavenly Father. Our Lord prayed that night in John 17 also for the unity of love and truth among His disciples, that their unity may be a living reflection in the world of the glory of the eternal love between the Father and the Son. Given that each and every Eucharist is a re-presentation of the death and Resurrection of Christ (see Lk 22:19; 1 Cor 11:23-26) and that Holy Communion is intended in part to strengthen those bonds of truth and love in His Church (see 1 Cor 10:16-17), the Eucharist may be said to manifest the glory of the love of God "for Himself," as Bl. Sopocko states: the love between the Father and the Son, manifested in the Paschal Mystery and in authentic ecclesial unity.

The Eucharist is a masterpiece of the love of Our Lord, the crown of all His inventions. It is, as it were, a big solar system in which love moves all, reaches with its rays to the end of all ages, and leads all creatures along the sunny road of love.

"Jesus, knowing that His hour had come to pass out of this world to the Father, having loved His own who were in the world, He loved them unto the end" (Jn 13:1).

II. We may consider the Eucharist either as a work of love or as a work of Mercy. If we regard our Lord in His human nature, we attribute the Eucharist rather to His love for us. If we consider Jesus as God, we see in the Eucharist rather His Mercy, for God's love for us is actually Mercy (see chapter 8: *Mercy of God, Unfathomable Love of the Sanctifier*). The Eucharist is the confirmation, substance, and enlargement of all that the Divine Mercy has created for us. To verify this statement let us consider the effects brought about by the Eucharist in the soul, and the fact that these effects are wrought by the Sacrament with complete gratuity, without regard for our worth or preparation,[50] despite our lukewarmness and all our past abuses of Jesus' love and confidence.

The effect of Holy Communion is the conservation and increase of sanctifying grace and supernatural life to a degree that is not attained by any other Sacrament. As bodily food serves to build the physical side of human beings, so the Blessed Sacrament revives and heals, protects and strengthens, feeds and develops the supernatural life of the soul. Here is effected the closest union with Christ, not only a spiritual

---

[50] Blessed Sopocko evidently means here that these sacramental "effects," (that is, sacramental graces) are freely offered to all the faithful who come to receive this Sacrament, but whether or not the graces offered will be received by us to our benefit obviously depends on the disposition of the soul at the time of Holy Communion. Only if we receive our Lord in a state of grace, with trustful surrender to His merciful love, can the Blessed Sacrament accomplish within us all that our Lord longs to do for us. In other words, charity and grace increase in the soul with the worthy reception of the Eucharist, that is, when we are first in a state of grace before receiving Holy Communion. The amount of that increase of grace, however, will be affected by the dispositions (such as faith and love) and the fervor with which we receive the Sacrament.

but also a physical union with such tangibility and perfection that no closer union on earth is possible. Moreover, this Sacrament has an extraordinary efficacy insofar as it imparts to us a special grace of devotion and of ardent love from which come happiness and bliss, peace and fortitude, and boundless readiness for sacrifices for God and our neighbor. The Eucharist also gives us actual grace that safeguards us from the fall into sin, which might be caused by persistent temptations, and takes away venial sins directly (*ex opere operato*) and indirectly (*ex opera operantis*). Finally, it produces a most welcome influence on the body and sensual appetite by checking disorderly passions, as the Evangelist attests: "And all the crowd were trying to touch him, for power went forth from him, and healed all" (Lk 6:19). Whence the Eucharist is rightly called "the wine bringing forth chastity." The incomparable beauty of the Catholic Church is a flower and fruit of the mystery of the Holy Eucharist.

The effects of the Eucharist are most clear proof that the infinite Mercy of God is there present, for the Lord works with such freedom and gratuity and only by reason of His boundless compassion for human wretchedness. "Let us therefore draw near with confidence to the throne of grace, that we may obtain mercy, and find grace to help in time of need" (Heb 4:16).

With faith and confidence, love and humility, joy and longing I will approach the Table of the Lord, the seat of graces and source of Mercy. I will confess that I am but as dust beneath the feet of the King Who is enthroned in my heart. "Jesus, I trust in You."

Chapter 27

MERCY OF GOD, GRANTED IN THE SACRAMENT OF THE PRIESTHOOD

"Thou are a priest for ever according to the order of Melchisedech"

— Psalm 109 [110]:4

I. Wherever there is a sacrifice, there also must be a priest. Christ in His human nature received the priesthood at the Incarnation, fulfilled His priestly office on the Cross, and now continues it in Heaven, transmitting to the faithful in the Mass the fruits of His sacrifice on the Cross. The Savior handed down the priestly power and the grace needed for its exercise to the apostles and their successors, the bishops and the priests, partly at the Last Supper and partly after His Resurrection when He gave them the power to forgive sins. All the [Eastern] churches that in the most remote times fell away from unity with Rome still have a priesthood and consider it to be the Sacrament instituted by Christ. No other truth is so clearly expressed in Scripture as this, that Christ imparted the priestly power to the apostles alone: "As the Father has sent me, I also send you" (Jn 20:21); "He who hears you hears me" (Lk 10:16); "Whatever you shall bind upon earth, shall be bound also in heaven" (Mt 18:18). They alone must feed the lambs (Jn 21:15), must be the foundation of the Church (Jn 17:18), and must constitute its government (Mt 18:17).

II. The priesthood is a manifestation of God's great Mercy toward the whole Church in general and toward priests in particular.

There are three activities of a priest by which God's Mercy flows out on the world: (1) sacrifice, (2) prayer, and (3) administration of the Sacraments and teaching.

The offering of Sacrifice is the main act of the priestly vocation, for here the priest is seen in all splendor and majesty as a mediator between God and the world. This is so with any sacrifice but especially with the sacrifice of the New Testament. In all truth, Christ Himself, the God-Man, is the sacrificial Victim as well as the invisible High Priest of the New Testament; but the priest is His visible representative and, as such, he really performs the act of the sacrifice of the Holy Mass from which ineffable benefits flow on the whole Church, and even on the whole world. The sacrifice of the Body and Blood of Christ is the soul and culmination of all devotion, the most important act of religion, in which God's sovereignty and man's dependence are given adequate expression.

The second function of the priest is prayer, which on the one hand is an act of worship and service to God, and on the other hand constitutes a most necessary means for obtaining divine grace. Prayer is a golden ladder by which adoration and thanksgiving mount up to God and the infinite Mercy of God descends. The Church puts the priest under obligation of saying certain prayers, determined strictly as to number, form, and time of recitation. These are the prayers of the Breviary, which for the most part is composed of psalms. The priests are the mouth of the Church, Christ's Spouse, through which she raises up a continuous, pure, and powerful prayer penetrating the heavens and bringing a merciful shower of graces on all people.

The third function of the priestly power that draws down on the faithful the special Mercy of God is the administration of the Sacraments and teaching. Here the goodness of God is revealed in the highest degree, because not only do the Sacraments help us to obtain temporal benefits, but through them the faithful receive or increase in themselves the precious gift of Heaven, sanctifying grace, and also a special right to actual graces in every situation of life from the cradle to the grave.

Through these functions of His priests Christ continues to be physically present among us, to pour down on us His Mercy, just as He did during His life on earth, and to teach and govern us.

III. What great Mercy God shows to His priests, whom He chooses from the faithful, not because of any merits of their own, but only because of His compassion on them! "You have not chosen me, but I have chosen you" (Jn 15:16). He calls them to take His place on earth. He entrusts them with His mysteries. They are, by His institution, the teachers of His doctrine, representatives of His power, mediators between God and humankind, and instruments whereby rich graces are won and supernatural operations effected. What an honor is brought to them and what an exalted dignity they possess by the fact that they are allowed to cooperate in God's work of saving souls and of redeeming the world! What a beautiful decree of the Divine Goodness! How great an honor Divine Mercy confers on those who are His messengers, from humanity to God and from God to humanity!

We should thank the Merciful Jesus for the benefits left to us all in the Sacrament of Holy Orders. Let us respect and love the representatives of His Power and Mercy and develop a deep appreciation for the sacrifice, the prayer, the Sacraments, and the teaching that we receive from them. Let us ask God to give us good and saintly priests. We ourselves can participate in the priesthood of Christ through offering ourselves to God through Him, and with Him, and in Him.[51]

---

[51] Blessed Sopocko alludes here not only to the liturgical offering of ourselves to God through Christ in the Holy Eucharist ("Through Him, with Him, and in Him"), but also to the daily, sacrificial offering of our life and labors to the Lord, as each day we live out our baptismal vocation to holiness and the Eucharistic mystery; as St. Paul wrote: "I appeal to you therefore, brethren, by the mercies of God, to present your bodies as a living sacrifice, holy and acceptable to God, which is your spiritual worship" (Rom 12:1), and "Walk in love, as Christ loved us and gave himself up for us, a fragrant offering and sacrifice to God" (Eph 5:2).

Chapter 28

MERCY OF GOD,
SHOWN IN CALLING US
TO THE HOLY FAITH

"He who does not believe shall be condemned"
— Mark 16:16

I. Faith is the primary basis of our relation to God as Christians, for through faith our union with God is effected: "Without faith it is impossible to please God" (Heb 11:6). All the supernatural life of the soul is based on the belief that Jesus Christ is God. This faith was required by the Savior from all who approached Him. This was a necessary condition of His miracles: "Let it be done to you according to your faith" (Mt 9:29). Faith can prevail on God to grant even what He did not intend primarily to concede, as we can see from the example of the Canaanite woman. Christ merited for us the unlimited treasures of grace for our salvation and left them to the Catholic Church, which alone teaches us the true faith. "One Lord, one faith, one baptism. One God and Father of all" (Eph 4:5-6). Here St. Paul indicates that because the true Church can be only one, we cannot afford to be indifferent amid multiple and conflicting creeds.

The Son of God bestowed on the Church marks so outstanding that anybody can discern them. They are so characteristic and evident that those who inquire and seek the truth with goodwill cannot fail to recognize them. Reason itself shows that the true Church must be only *one*; *of Apostolic origin* with an unbroken continuity; *universal,* i.e., common and changeless for all people and all ages; and *holy*, that is, it must possess the effective means of sanctification on earth and really sanctify men and women, and lead them to Heaven. Such is the Catholic Church alone. It is one because it has always taught the same truths of the Christian faith. It is Catholic, which means universal, for it extends its benefits to all nations. It is apostolic, since it reaches directly to apostolic times. Finally, it is holy in that it always sanctifies people and God attests to this by miracles. The Church essentially dates from the time of the earthly Paradise,[52] and it will prevail as the Church triumphant not only to the end of the world, but through all eternity: "And I will espouse thee to Me in Mercy" (Hos 2:19).

II. God's Mercy summoned us out of the multitude of innumerable infidels and heretics and called us to the true holy faith. First of all, we are indebted to God's Mercy for being born, not in pre-Christian times when there was a dearth of the heavenly gifts, but even now, in the golden age of grace. The Merciful Jesus preceded us with graces and created our souls when Satan was already defeated, death conquered, Heaven opened, Divine Mercy revealed, and the straight road to Heaven clearly shown. Truly, this is the golden age of grace, since at any time the sinner can easily repair the faults of his whole life. Divine Mercy descends on us more plentifully than snowflakes in the winter. It comes to us like the fragrance of the innumerable flowers in springtime. However, even in this time of grace a countless number of people remain in heresy or godlessness. We have, by God's Mercy, received Baptism in His Church, learned the principles of the true faith, and profited by the means of sanctification.

Let us not think that all this happened by mere chance, for as the inspired author says, the Lord has "ordered all things in measure, and number, and weight" (Wis 11:21).

---

[52] By "the earthly Paradise" Bl. Sopocko here means the Garden of Eden. In this he follows the early Fathers of the Church, who taught that the assembly of the faithful by divine grace, the "church" of the Old Testament, began with Adam and Eve, and continued in God's Chosen People, Israel. The Catholic Church is simply the Body of the New Adam, and the community of the spiritually renewed Israel.

Like the lepers cleansed by Christ, we do not always remember to be grateful to God for calling us to the true and holy faith. From now on, let our gratitude be fervent and full of love, humble, and respectful for all the truths of our holy faith as well as submissive to the teaching Church.

I will profess my faith with fortitude always and everywhere. I will give thanks for the gift of faith. I will venerate the Mercy of God.

Chapter 29

MERCY OF GOD, REVEALED IN THE CONVERSION OF SINNERS

"Take courage, son, thy sins are forgiven thee"
— Matthew 9:2

I. How tender are the words of the Holy Scripture that tell of the Divine Mercy for sinners. Despite their malice, stubbornness, and perversity God spares, guards, and protects them while waiting patiently for their conversion. Sorrowful at their blindness He hastens to help the wretched and uses all means to bring them to their senses. Next, He resorts to severity and punishment to pierce their hard hearts. Finally, He does not keep those waiting for long before the threshold of His grace who are sorry for offending Him; He does not reproach them for their past ingratitude; He does not remember their blunders, but forgives them in a moment. "He hath not dealt with us according to our sins: nor rewarded us according to our iniquities. For according to the height of the heaven above the earth: He hath strengthened His Mercy toward them that fear Him" (Ps 102 [103]: 10-11).

God in various ways desires to touch the heart of the sinner. Thus He gives benefits, inspirations, and grace, and He reproaches the troubled conscience. If these measures fail and the sinner thoughtlessly persists in his unhappy state, the Father of Mercy is not disheartened by this stubbornness but pours bitterness into his unlawful delights, and cries out to him in the examples of the punishments of others. He does not leave and abandon the sinner, nor does He ever rest, since

He can never exhaust all the treasures of His Mercy. This is exemplified by the unworthy Judas, whose feet Jesus washed, whom He fed with His Body, whom He called His friend and favored with the kiss of love. After these and all the other graces given to Judas, He did not inflict vengeance and punishment on him, but sorrowed because of his blindness: "He was troubled in spirit" (Jn 13:21).

Sometimes God has recourse to severity, but His chastisement is mainly directed to bringing those going astray to their senses and thwarting their sinful intentions. Many times He seems to crush sinners without pity like earthen pots but He does so only that, regenerated in soul, they might rise from the ruins and become chosen vessels like St. Paul. "But when we are judged, we are being chastised by the Lord that we may not be condemned with this world" (1 Cor 11:32).

II. The soul, brought to contrition by God's benignity or punishment, rises from the fall at last. Then, instead of anger and bitter reproaches the Heavenly Father welcomes the penitent, and joyfully invites the angelic choirs to rejoice in the return of the lost sheep. "Rejoice with me, because I have found my sheep that was lost" (Lk 15:6).

Who would believe that the Lord also has His days, the days of special joy on which He seems to be more happy than usual? When does the Lord feel such joy? Is it when people render Him glory, when they build sanctuaries to Him, when the martyrs give their life for His Name? No doubt, God rejoices in all that. But the summit of His joy is the conversion of the sinner. It is the day of gladness for God when the sinful man abandons his sordid life and washes himself with tears of sorrow for having offended God; when the extortioner, the usurer, and the wrongdoer stop their malice and, like Zacheus, compensate [their victims] in a fourfold manner for the wrongs committed against them; when the fickle and fallen woman rises from her degradation and, like Magdalen, becomes a penitent; when any sinner amends his way of life.

Not only does God willingly forgive the prodigal sons who do penance, but He also soothes the wounds of their hearts, pours solace into each soul, presents them with festive garments by restoring their innocence and adopting them as His children. Upon the lamentable ruin of sin, He raises a new sanctuary of the regenerated soul. He clothes it with the garment of sanctifying grace, adorns it with a crown of His gifts, restores its lost merits and its right to Heaven. "And I will bring them back again, because I will have Mercy on them: and they shall be as they were when I had cast them off, for I am the Lord their God, and will hear them. And their heart shall rejoice as through wine, and their heart shall be joyful in the Lord ... because I have redeemed them" (Zech 10:6-8).

Let us cherish the sweet and infinite kindness of our Heavenly Father. God has often showed His Mercy to us as He showed it to Magdalen, Zacheus, Peter, Saul, the thief on the cross whom He favored with His grace even at the last moment of his life, and many others. Let us have confidence in Him and do penance for our faults.

Chapter 30

MERCY OF GOD, MANIFESTED IN THE SANCTIFICATION OF THE JUST

*"That we may be now no longer children,
tossed to and fro ... Rather are we to ... grow up in
all things in Him Who is the head, Christ."*

— Ephesians 4:14-15

I. The state of grace makes a person just. The just man should not stand at the border of sin but must grow and progress in virtues, must sanctify himself, "to grow up in Him Who is the head, Christ," as St. Paul says. Each person's sanctification is the work both of God's Mercy and of our personal cooperation.

While we are children, Divine Mercy pours on us the graces of justification and adoption [in Baptism] without any active participation on our part; but as soon as we reach the age of reason, God's Mercy requires our cooperation. "Turn ye to Me, saith the Lord of hosts: and I will turn to you" (Zech 1:3). No one will become a saint unless he himself wishes to be one. God anticipates his efforts with grace but he has to submit himself to its operation and convert himself by faith, hope, penance, and love, using all the means that God has established for his sanctification and growth in grace, which flows from His Mercy.[53]

---

[53] The relationship between grace and free will is a deep mystery, but the Catholic Church has set some parameters for understanding it, to the extent that we can, and Bl. Sopocko certainly means to abide by those guidelines here. In a nutshell, God's grace aims to enable our cooperation. Our cooperation, too, is therefore a fruit of His grace at work within us. The matter is summed up in the editor's book, *Divine*

We are obliged to keep the commandments of God and of the Church, and to fulfill the duties of our state of life. If this depended on our own strength, we could not fulfill these obligations. It is a dogma of faith that by our own strength, we certainly could not fulfill these obligations. It is a dogma of faith that by our own strength we are unable to keep all

---

Mercy: A Guide from Genesis to Benedict XVI (Stockbridge: Marian Press, revised edition, 2009), p. 105-107:

It is ... a defined doctrine of the Catholic Church (both at the Western Council of Orange in 529 and at the 16th century ecumenical Council of Trent), that no one can turn to God for saving help or do anything at all toward salvation unless prompted, strengthened, and assisted to do so every step of the way by God's grace. On the other hand, God's saving grace is not irresistible. He certainly *enables* our response of faith and love to Him, but He never *compels* that response. To put it another way: setting a person free from bondage in prison and giving him a helping hand to start a new life on the outside does not guarantee that the person will use his new freedom wisely and that he will not end up back in prison again. Yet unless we are first set free by God's enabling grace from our bondage to our fallen condition, we have no capacity freely to cooperate with His grace and attain salvation.

The Catholic Tradition sees two equal and opposite dangers. On the one hand there is "Quietism" and classical "Calvinism": the doctrine that human beings are merely passive under the sway of God's saving grace, which is essentially irresistible. ... On the other hand there is "Pelagianism": the doctrine that we do not need God's saving grace within; we can just save ourselves by our own efforts by striving to follow the good example of Jesus and the saints. A variant of this is known as "Semi-Pelagianism": the doctrine that while we do indeed need the help of God's grace within our souls, we do not always need God to take the initiative with His enabling grace. As some Eastern theologians have taught (for example, John Cassian), sometimes we freely reach out to God first, and He responds to us, or our seeking of Him meets His seeking of us in a simultaneous "synergy." But all of these doctrines violate some part of the Catholic Tradition that we have received from St. Paul, Orange, and Trent, one that St. Bernard [of Clairvaux] ... summed up for us in his treatise *On Grace and Free Will*:

It is this grace which arouses free choice when it sows the seed of the good thought, which heals free choice by changing its disposition, which strengthens it so as to lead it to action, and which saves it from experiencing a fall. Grace so cooperates with free choice, however, that only in the first movement does it go a step ahead of it. In the others it accompanies it. Indeed, grace's whole aim in taking a step ahead is that from then on, free choice may co-operate with it. What was begun by grace alone is completed by grace and free choice together ... (*On Grace and Free Will*, 46).

the commandments of God, still less persevere in the state of grace until death. We have been expressly told by our Savior that "without Me you can do nothing" (Jn 15:5). Therefore, we must always pray and hope for God's merciful assistance. Perseverance is a special gift of Divine Mercy, but it does not exclude our cooperation; on the contrary, it supposes our cooperation. "Strive even more, by good works to mark your calling and election sure" (2 Pet 1:10).

A considerable number of our salutary acts are given to defending our souls against interior and exterior enemies, called "the concupiscence of the body, of the eyes and the pride of life." "The life of every human being upon earth is a warfare" (Job 7:1). Divine Mercy helps and supports us in this combat; nevertheless, on our part vigilance, prayer, and much effort are needed. "Watch and pray, that you may not enter into temptation" (Mt 26:41).

II. We distinguish two kinds of actual graces: those which make it entirely possible for us to do something good, but which remain without result because of our neglect in cooperating with them; and those with which we cooperate. We know very well that we don't want to cooperate with some graces; these are called "sufficient graces." To the others we are docile, and these are called "efficacious graces." God complains in the Holy Scripture that His voice is not being heard (Jer 7:13) and admonishes us not to receive His graces in vain: "We entreat you not to receive the grace of God in vain" (2 Cor 6:1).

Although our free will decides and is a necessary condition in the acquisition of merit, the difference between sufficient and efficacious grace comes rather from God. He has, from all ages, foreseen the graces with which we will cooperate, and those which we will reject. A good act depends, therefore, on God, Who provides the individual with the efficacious graces for its performance, and it also depends on the person himself, who cooperates with these graces conferred on him precisely in view of his cooperation.[54]

---

[54] In this paragraph, using terminology drawn from St. Augustine, Bl. Sopocko adopts one of the ways of understanding St. Paul's teaching on the mystery of

Sufficient graces conferred on all people are themselves a manifestation of the infinite Mercy of God and prove that God "wishes all men to be saved" (1 Tim 2:4). A clearer witness to God's Mercy is efficacious grace, which we cannot merit, but which we can only prepare ourselves for by prayer and by avoiding everything that displeases God. These are, as it were, a whole series of victorious graces that enlighten, attract, and comfort us; defend us in temptations; and accompany us until our death. Perseverance is an efficacious grace that is above all other graces. When we consider it, we face the unfathomable mystery of God's Mercy, which chooses the elect by conferring on them efficacious auxiliary graces and by sanctifying them.

Mindful of Saul, Magdalen, Augustine, and other great sinners whose most stubborn nature was overcome by efficacious grace, I will rely on this grace in conquering myself, in the struggle against temptations and in the performance of virtuous acts. I will ardently pray for it and thank God for previous help.

---

predestination and election that are permissible for Catholic theologians to hold: namely, that God bestows upon souls some graces that actually will result in their full sanctification and salvation ("efficacious graces"), because He foresees that those souls will freely cooperate with those saving graces if He gives them such help. On that basis, while God mercifully grants at least some graces ("sufficient graces") to all souls, He bestows the graces of salvation only upon some, "the elect," rather than others. This perspective on predestination, drawn from one of the streams of the Augustinian tradition of theology, has never been taught definitively by the Catholic Church, and leads to the obvious question: What are those sufficient graces "sufficient" for if they cannot actually lead anyone to salvation? Some theologians today follow instead the teachings of St. Francis de Sales: that the sufficient graces bestowed in some way on all souls are "sufficient" to save any soul, if only the soul chooses to cooperate with them — in which case we call them "efficacious graces." Saint Alphonsus de Liguori further defined those sufficient graces from God as the grace given to us all to pray, and to ask for God's saving help.

Chapter 31

MERCY OF GOD,
FULFILLED IN THE PERFECTING
OF THE SAINTLY

"It is now no longer I that live,
but Christ lives in me"

— Galatians 2:20

I. God often imparts Himself to humanity in an extraordinary manner.

He is more alive in each person's soul than the person himself, who should cooperate with God always. While the influence of ordinary grace is not always noticeable, this extraordinary activity of God manifests itself outwardly quite clearly and perceptibly, at least in regard to him in whom it is taking place. This exceptional influence of God causes a magnificent development of the virtues, which reach a heroic degree. This is the way in which the perfection of the saintly souls is usually accomplished.

The term "sanctity," in its broadest sense, applies to all Christians in a state of grace. In the narrow sense, we apply it to those who not only are in the state of sanctifying grace, but have reached heroism in all the important virtues of the Christian life (theological and moral),[55] and those proper to one's state), who devote their lives to practicing these virtues, and whose sanctity becomes distinguished by miracles either before or after death. (However, only the miracles occurring

---

[55] The "moral" virtues (also known as "cardinal" virtues, that is, virtues on which the moral life are founded) are prudence, justice, fortitude, and temperance (see *Catechism*, entries 1804-1809).

after death are sufficient evidence for the Church in the canonization procedure.)

A saint is a Christian in whom the beauty and grandeur of the supernatural life and evangelical perfection have been manifested, in whom grace has achieved the highest triumphs, in whom the virtues have produced their choicest fruit, and in whom the gifts of Mercy have brought about all that God intended. A saint, in the supernatural sphere, is like the hero, the genius, or "the great," in the proper sense of the word. The power of God and human strength are wonderfully blended in a saint.

Canonization proceedings, which often continue for years, institute a very detailed, strict, and thorough investigation of the virtues and miracles of the holy person. Only after the process is finished does there follow an official pronouncement of the Church that the virtues of this holy person really reached a degree of heroism, that his (or her) miracles were authentic, and that public prayers may be offered to that person, since that person is worthy to be raised to the altar as a saint. Then only do we on earth know who is a saint in Heaven. But how many real saints there are, whom we shall not know until we are in eternity!

II. The perfection of a saintly person is the work of Divine Mercy to a special degree. If God is the principal author of the conversion of sinners, how much more must the life of a saint be His work, since in it the entire greatness and splendor of His merciful graces are developed. He chose the saint, still hidden in his mother's womb, and planned for him a magnificent flight without any merits of his own. God made him His adopted child through sanctifying grace, then increased this grace; protected him against dangers; and, if His gifts were lost by sin, He restored them through His Sacraments.

Indeed, nothing but God's Mercy rears and directs the saints in this marvelous way. It fills the mind of the youth with the light of understanding. It crushes the resistance of the evil inclinations, and under its influence the will becomes noble, tender, and strong. It draws all the saints to a suitable field of action in the Church and in the world. It opens bountiful treasures of graces to its beloved sons and daughters, and shines on their earthly lives with the brightness of its spiritual gifts.

"Behold I will bring upon her (Jerusalem, which here represents the soul) as it were a river of peace, and as an overflowing torrent the glory of the Gentiles ... ; you shall be carried at the breasts, and upon the knees they shall caress you. As one whom the mother caresseth, so will I comfort you" (Is 66:12-13). The saints attest to the truth of this prophecy. Saint Thérèse of the Child Jesus, for instance, says, "Never have I been consoled by words more tender and more sweet. O Jesus! Thy arms, then, are the elevator which must raise me even unto Heaven" (*The Story of a Soul*).

Finally, Divine Mercy awakens among the faithful a great, sudden, and inexplicable impulse to honor and trust some chosen soul. This public response to sanctity occurs in various places and becomes one of the main causes for the canonization of this soul.

Saint Francis de Sales, at the canonization of St. Francis Xavier, cried out: "Here is the third Francis elevated to the altars! I want to be the fourth." He kept his words, and Divine Mercy crowned his desires. We should all tend to sanctity and, above all else, desire to become saints, though we should not wish for the honor of canonization.

COMMENTARY:
THE MERCIFUL GOD DELIVERS
US FROM DESPAIR

As a seasoned spiritual director, Bl. Michael Sopocko was no stranger to the human struggle against spiritual desolation, and even against despair.

In fact, the most devout Christians — even great saints such as St. Teresa of Calcutta and St. Thérèse of Lisieux, the Little Flower — sometimes experience strong temptations to give up hope. Some have gone through many months, even years, of spiritual desolation: a journey through the spiritual wilderness in which they felt that God was far away. They certainly did not despair, but they were grievously tempted to do so. Although our Lord did not succumb to despair either, He passed through an unfathomable desolation of spirit when He cried out on the Cross, "My God, my God, why have you forsaken me?" (Mt 27:46; Mk 15:34)

Blessed Sopocko reflects on the causes of outright despair in *God is Mercy*, chapter 34:

> The causes of despair can vary: Temporal or spiritual misfortunes, incurable illness, loss of respect and of honor, financial ruin, threat of inevitable danger, etc. Under the influence of such disasters there follows a terrible depression, which takes away all energy, paralyzes the nerves, renders clear thinking impossible, and even impedes breathing and the normal circulation of the blood, so that the brain is not supplied sufficiently with oxygen and ceases to function efficiently. ... If we search for the very first, deepest cause of despair, we always find a lack of trust in the Mercy of God.

When racked by grief and misfortunes, some people would be tempted to fire back: "Is it any wonder I find it hard to trust in Him? Just look at what trials and tribulations He has permitted to happen to me! How can I trust a God who treats me this way?"

This is similar to Job's protest in the Old Testament when he complained bitterly to God about the suffering he and his family had endured. We need to remember that although Job got it wrong, he was actually *commended* by God for his honesty. God was pleased that Job refused to accept the facile, pious platitudes of his friends ("If God is making you suffer so much, it must be because you are an especially big sinner") or the temptation to despair from his wife ("Just curse God and die").

Then what did Job get wrong? He forgot that his own knowledge was finite and God's wisdom is infinite (see Is 55:8-9). If God permits us to go through times of seemingly impenetrable darkness, we have to trust that, since He is infinitely wise and we are not, He knows the reason why it is best to permit such trials, even if we cannot yet see that reason ourselves.

To be sure, God does not always do what we would like Him to do, or what we think He ought to do. Nevertheless, it is presumptuous and spiritually dangerous to insist that God must act in ways which we consider good, and that if He does not, we will lose our love and respect for Him. After all, God has the ability to see the "big picture"; we mostly see just our immediate needs. The Protestant author Dan Story has written that, at least in this present life:

> [W]e will never fully understand why God chooses to act as He does in many situations, or why He allows events to happen that seem inconsistent with His character. Nevertheless, although much of what God does is a mystery, we do have His assurance that what He does is ultimately in the best interest of those who believe in Him. If we know

God, we will learn to trust Him, even if we do not
fully understand what He is doing (*Defending Your
Faith*, 1997, p. 16).

From the Old Testament, Bl. Sopocko cites the example
of King David, who wrestled with this matter of trust in God
throughout his life:

> The poor shepherd David goes forth to battle
> against the well-equipped Philistine giant, whom
> he defeats because he trusted in God's help. "Thou
> comest to me with a sword, and with a spear, and
> with a shield: but I come to thee in the name of
> the Lord of Hosts" (I Sam 17:45). This same David
> reproaches himself in other instances for excessive
> fear, and for a lack of trust in God. "Why art thou
> sad, O my soul? And why dost thou trouble me?
> Hope in God" (Ps 41:6 [42:5]). "Therefore will I
> not fear when the earth shall be troubled and the
> mountains shall be removed into the heart of the
> sea" (Ps 45 [46]:2) (*God is Mercy*, chapter 3).

In other words, we need not give in to despair even when
the world seems to be turning upside down with troubles
and sorrows. Almighty God would not permit such things to
happen unless it was at least possible for good to come out of
them, if we cooperate with His grace — indeed, sometimes a
good even greater than if He had not permitted these things
to happen in the first place! That is why St. Paul wrote: "All
things work together unto good for them that love God"
(Rom 8:28).

It is not that good will *always* arise from divinely permitted suffering, or that everything will *automatically* turn
out for the best for everyone; it is possible only for those who
"love God," St. Paul says, and the first and most fundamental
way we can love Him is to trust in His merciful love for us.
For to trust in Him is lovingly to give to Him the thing He
most wants: the very depths of our hearts. When we do that,

it opens the door to all the graces and blessings He wants to pour out on us.

Our Lord invites us to trust in Him, Bl. Sopocko says, as sheep trust in the leading of their shepherd without knowing the path ahead themselves:

> Through the most tender words and pictures does Jesus call to the soul to follow Him with childlike simplicity and trust. "I am," He says, "The Good Shepherd" (Jn 10:11) and it is this title that should awaken boundless trust in every heart. ... He likens Himself to a Good Shepherd, Who knows and loves His flock, feeding it with grace, with doctrine, and with His most Holy Body and Blood. ... Would our Redeemer so indefatigably encourage us to trust in Him, if He did not want to reward this trust with Mercy? ... Jesus, I trust in You. I trust that You will forgive my sins and that You have prepared Heaven for me. I trust that You will provide all the graces I need to save my soul (*God is Mercy*, chapter 3).

This last point is especially important. One of the reasons why people often slide into despair is that they assume that the goal of life on this earth is our "happiness." (After all, doesn't the United States' Declaration of Independence tell us we have the right to pursue happiness? Since such a right is ingrained in us, it does not seem unreasonable to many of us to turn to God saying: "If I have done everything within my power to pursue happiness, then You *ought* to grant it to me!") God certainly doesn't want us to be continually miserable in this life. But His first goal for us on this planet is not our temporal *happiness* — in other words, not our comfort, health, happy family, and financial security, with everything in our lives going fairly well, etc. Rather, His first goal for us is our *holiness*, our sanctification, the transformation of our souls in repentance, faith, and love, because it is only souls like this that can share His infinite joy and eternal life with Him in Heaven.

As we so easily let our hearts become possessed with lesser things, is it any wonder that God often lets these lesser things be taken away from us along our life's journey? C.S. Lewis put it this way in his book *The Problem of Pain* (chapter 7):

> We are never safe, but we have plenty of fun, and some ecstasy. It is not hard to see why. The security we crave would teach us to rest our hearts in this world and oppose an obstacle to our return to God: a few moments of happy love, a landscape, a symphony, a merry meeting with our friends, a bathe, or a football match, have no such tendency. Our Father refreshes us on the journey with some pleasant inns, but will not encourage us to mistake them for home.

Above all, what God wants to give us is the fullness of sanctity, and the very best possible preparation for eternal life. Although His ways of doing so sometimes seem incomprehensible to us, we can trust Him in the midst of trouble and sorrow to provide for us what *He* knows we most need, and not just what *we* think we need most. Blessed Sopocko invites us to do just that:

> I know that God wills my sanctity, that He acts for this end, and that He possesses a thousand means to bring it about. Joys and sorrows, light and darkness, consolation and dryness, health and sickness — all this is for my salvation. So I will follow Your advice, O Merciful Savior, which You gave to St. Gertrude: "Make an act of giving yourself to My good pleasure that I may freely dispose of everything concerning you. ... In all unite your sentiments with the sentiments of My most merciful Heart!" (*God is Mercy*, chapter 43)

Chapter 32

MERCY OF GOD, FOUNT OF HEALTH FOR THE SICK AND SUFFERING

"I overflow with joy in all our troubles"
— 2 Corinthians 7:4

I. The temporal life of humanity is filled not with smiles only, but with pains, diseases, and afflictions. "Man born of woman, living for a short time, is filled with many miseries" (Job 14:1). Even our Savior included physical pain in the program of Redemption, saying to the disciples, "No disciple is above his teacher" (Lk 6:40). Physical pain brings tears to our eyes, and most people avoid pain or suffer with resistance and loathing, and consequently without any relief or merit.

Disease is the result of original sin,[56] and the sufferings accompanying disease are a penance for it. "Sin no more, lest something worse befall thee" (Jn 5:14), said Jesus to the cured paralytic. The Savior pitied the sick and cured them. He said of Himself to the disciples of St. John the Baptist, "Go and report to John what you have heard and seen: the blind see, the lame walk, the lepers are cleansed, the deaf hear" (Lk 7:22). Nowadays, too, Jesus cures the sick in numerous miraculous places, and because of this He may be rightly called a fount of cures for the sick and suffering.

---

[56] Blessed Sopocko does not necessarily insist here that disease microbes in the biosphere are caused to exist by original sin. Rather (in accord with the decree on original sin of the Council of Trent), he is concerned to make the point that humanity itself became subject to disease, suffering, and death as a result of the fall from grace of the first parents of the human race, Adam and Eve, in a way that God, our good Creator, never intended.

The sickness of the soul is, however, more painful and more serious than the illness of the body, and the reproaches of conscience often greatly exceed physical suffering. They undermine the health of the body; weaken the strength, firmness, and fortitude of the soul; destroy its peace and hamper its flight to God. Furthermore, they make the soul morose and enclosed within itself, irritable, and ill-disposed to others. They deprive it of eagerness to pray, desire to work, and readiness to carry on the spiritual struggle, and sometimes even incite the soul to new transgressions.

Our Lord gave us, for this kind of disease of the soul, a wonderful remedy in the Sacrament of Penance. "Go in peace and sin no more" are the words spoken to the penitent by Christ's representative. Our hearts melt at the very memory of this, tears come to our eyes, and a blissful feeling penetrates our souls. Truly this Sacrament is the fount of cures for the sick and suffering. Even physicians witness the improvement of health in the sick who made a good confession.

II. Moreover, diseases and the sufferings flowing from them are for us not an insignificant benefit of the Divine Mercy. The diseases tear us away from sin and direct us to God by purifying the soul of its imperfections and making it sensitive to the influence of God's grace. The conversion of many saints has occurred during their illness: for example, St. Ignatius Loyola, St. Camillo de Lellis, and many others.

Disease is a school for the soul because it shows us how powerful is God, Who can humiliate the proud in one moment. It teaches us the weakness of human beings, who live but a short time amidst many sufferings; the gravity of sin, which has brought disease and other punishments in its wake; and the value of Heaven, since one has to pay so much for the privilege of entering it.

Finally, disease is a source of merit for the soul, for through it one can make up for the temporal punishment [due to one's sins] and earn a high degree of heavenly glory. Furthermore, one can offer up one's suffering for the souls in Purgatory, or for the conversion of sinners.

However, even for perfect souls disease is not easy to endure, especially when it is irritating and prolonged. Then, it scarcely sanctifies many, for disease of the soul often follows sickness of the body — as shown in complaints about the nurses, about the disease itself, and even against God; and in irritability and exaggerated solicitude for the body. In order to profit by disease one should willingly suffer with Christ: "That I may live to God. With Christ I am nailed to the cross" (Gal 2:19-20). We feel more courage in our sickness when we behold the Cross and draw near to the [wounded] side of Christ. When suffering mounts, let us recall His words: "Blessed are they who mourn ... Blessed are they who suffer" (Mt 5:4 and 10). This thought soothes pain and reminds us of our reward in Heaven. So the Merciful Jesus, also in this respect, becomes a fount of cures for the sick and the suffering.

I will accept sufferings without murmuring and treat them as my Purgatory on earth and as my trial from God, destined for me from eternity. I will ask God to give me the grace to suffer in Christ: "When my strength shall fail, do not thou forsake me" (Ps 70 [71]:9). I will entrust my illness with all its pains to the holy Will of God. "Jesus, I trust in You!"

Chapter 33

MERCY OF GOD,
SOLACE OF ANGUISHED HEARTS

*"Give not up thy soul to sadness,
and afflict not thyself in thy own counsel"*
— Sirach 30:21

I. Interior anguish comes from great sadness. According to St. Thomas, sadness is a feeling of distress, caused by the thought of something painful. We have a natural inclination to sadness. Sometimes it can result from a visitation of God or from Satanic temptation. Sadness in itself is neither good nor bad, but it becomes good or bad on account of the object that occasions it, and the degree to which it becomes evident.

The right kind of sadness comes from God. It is caused by the realization of our own misery, a recognition of our sins, compassion for the physical and spiritual misfortunes of others, our longing for God, and the thought that God is offended. The fruit of this sadness is the purification of the heart, abundant merit, and holy solace. "Blessed are they who mourn, for they shall be comforted" (Mt 5:4).

The wrong kind of sadness comes from immoderate regret at the loss of goods, consolations, and honors of the world; from offended pride and irritated self-love; from envy, greed, and humiliations.

This sadness is usually accompanied by irritability and anger toward others, and distrust of God. Sometimes, even devout people succumb to this sadness, and consequently they are unable to pray, to meditate, or to do good as they might wish.

The effects of inordinate sadness are dreadful, for they drive a man to the grave before his time. Like a black cloud such sadness surrounds the soul everywhere so that the rays of God's grace or human consolation cannot penetrate it. It makes the soul distrustful of God, and without trust the soul suffers and undergoes terrible interior torments. The Fathers of the Church rightly call this sadness "Satan's bath" or "the cave of the robbers," for Satan lies in wait in the cave of sadness like a robber; he strives to cause confusion and unrest in the soul; and finally he attacks the soul with all his strength. Sometimes, "even mortal sin does not give to Satan so much power over the soul as sadness" (Fr. Faber). "For sadness hath killed many, and there is no profit in it" (Sir 30:23). Sadness is the true anguish of the human heart.

II. "The joyfulness of the heart, is the life of man, and a never failing treasure of holiness" (Sir 30:22). It is the Merciful Jesus Who draws down this joyfulness on the soul. First of all, He calms a man who has the right kind of sadness by purifying his soul in the Sacrament of Penance and pouring into it sanctifying grace. He is powerful also in curing inordinate sadness, if only the sufferer will turn to Him with trust: "Is any one of you sad? Let him pray," says the Apostle (Jas 5:13). As a sunbeam disperses the fog, so prayer removes all kind of sadness. Whenever St. Ludgarde was sad, she kissed the wound of the Sacred Heart of Jesus with great fervor and immediately all bitterness changed into sweetness.

Sometimes sadness is a symptom of a tendency to disease or a direct effect of an actual disease. In this case one should undergo medical treatment, and use exterior means like reading good books, or gazing at a beautiful countryside. A change of abode, singing, the company of dear friends are efficacious too, but the most efficacious means is the company of our best friend, the Merciful Jesus, Who applies balm soothing all the wounds of the human heart.

Besides sadness another cause of interior anguish can be anxiety, that is, an inordinate wish for something or an

immoderate desire to get rid of some hardship. "Anxiety,"
says St. Francis de Sales, "is, after sin, the greatest evil, for
the dismayed and troubled heart loses strength needed for
preservation of the acquired virtues as well as for resisting
the enemy who tries to catch fishes in troubled waters." To
get rid of anxiety or to secure oneself against it, one should
avoid inordinate desires and attachments, restrain those
rising up, and always conform oneself to God's Will, which
is Mercy Itself. Also, one should overcome excessive activity
and precipitation in action, following the counsel of the Wise
Man: "There is a time and opportunity for every business"
(Eccl 8:6).

"Father, if Thou art willing, remove this cup from Me; yet not My will, but Thine be done" (Lk 22:42). O Lord, I will fulfill Your holy Will in my struggles and sufferings, in my joys and in my illnesses. I will seek relief in Your Mercy only. You, O Jesus, have given me an example in the Garden of Olives.

Chapter 34

MERCY OF GOD,
HOPE OF SOULS AFFLICTED
WITH DESPAIR

*"Gather up thy heart in holiness:
and drive away sadness far from thee"*
— Sirach 30:24

I. "Despair" is a passion arising in us because of the impossibility of escaping evil. The word covers not only the feeling of despair itself, but also the inclination to it. Despair exerts a very harmful influence on the human physical and spiritual condition. It is opposed to hope and trust — so much so, that while hope enlivens, despair kills. Cain, Judas, and numerous suicides even of our times serve to prove this fact.*

The causes of despair can vary: temporal or spiritual misfortunes, incurable illness, loss of respect and of honor, financial ruin, threat of inevitable danger, etc. Under the influence of such disasters there follows a terrible depression, which takes away all energy, paralyzes the nerves, renders clear thinking impossible, and even impedes breathing and normal circulation of the blood, so that the brain is not supplied sufficiently with oxygen and ceases to function efficiently. For instance, in despair a man begins to reason in this way: "God is infinitely just, and my sins are so great that there is no hope of my salvation." Thus, Cain reasoned:

---

* The Catholic Church does not teach that suicide is always a sign of sinful despair, since even though suicide is a gravely wrong act, it is also often not a fully free act (see *Catechism*, 2282-2283), and so would not be a mortal sin (see *Catechism*, 1857). For more on all this, see Fr. Chris Alar, MIC, and Br. Jason Lewis, MIC, *After Suicide: There's Hope for Them and for You* (Marian Press, 2019).

"My iniquity is greater than that I may deserve pardon" (Gen 4:13).

If we search for the very first, deepest cause of despair, we always find a lack of trust in the Mercy of God, a lack which often borders on an almost slavish fear of the Divine Justice, and many a time borders on complete disbelief. It is true that God is infinitely just and we must fear Him, but with a filial, not servile fear, a holy fear joined with trust in the infinite Mercy of God. It is true that sin is an evil even greater than we can imagine, but the greatest sin is not the one that is an occasion for despair, but the black infernal sin of despair itself. This is the greatest sin.[57]

II. "How great is the Mercy of the Lord and His forgiveness to them that turn to Him!" (Sir 17:28). Sin interposes an infinite distance between us and God, but penance leads us back to the Lord. God is indeed infinitely just, yet His Mercy surpasses His Justice. There is no sin that God cannot forgive. The prophet knew of the Divine Justice, yet, despite his sins, he trusted in Mercy, raised his eyes upward with emotion, and did not hesitate to sing, "His tender mercies are over all His works" (Ps 144 [145]:9).

When the sorrowing Jeremiah sat on the ruins of the Temple of Jerusalem and yielded to excessive sadness, the Lord consoled him: "There shall be heard again in this place the voice of joy and the voice of gladness, the voice of the bridegroom and the voice of the bride, the voice of them that

---

[57] By "[despair] is the greatest sin" Bl. Sopocko may be referring to the teaching of St. Thomas Aquinas (in *ST* 2a2ae, q. 20) that, seen from one angle, despair is the worst sin, because it is directly opposed to the theological virtue of hope. Seen from another angle, St. Thomas says, unbelief and hatred of God are even worse:

For unbelief is due to a man not believing God's own truth; while the hatred of God arises from man's will being opposed to God's goodness itself; whereas despair consists in a man ceasing to hope for a share of God's goodness. Hence it is clear that unbelief and hatred of God are against God as He is in Himself, while despair is against Him, according as His good is partaken of by us. Wherefore strictly speaking it is more grievous sin to disbelieve God's truth, or to hate God, than not to hope to receive glory from Him.

shall say, Give ye glory to the Lord of hosts, for the Lord is good, for His Mercy endureth for ever" (Jer 33:10-11). This promise is verified in the sinner also. His soul is the temple destroyed by Satan, but God raises a new temple up, regenerates the sinful soul, clothes it with the garment of sanctity, adorns it with the crown of grace, restores its merits and its right to heaven.[58]

"If your sins be as scarlet, they shall be made as white as snow: and if they be red as crimson, they shall be white as wool" (Is 1:18).

Let no one, then, say that there is no hope for him. There is hope for everyone, for the prophecies of the Old Testament concerning the Savior are already fulfilled and our altars contain the Blood of the Merciful Christ, Whose Spouse, the Church, proclaims to all people of goodwill: "I desire Mercy, and not sacrifice, for I have come to call sinners, not the just" (Mt 9:13). "There will be joy in heaven over one sinner that repents, more than over ninety-nine just who have no need of repentance" (Lk 15:7).

Let despair vanish, then, before the infinite Mercy of God. Let us stand firm against discouragement, which deprives us of vital energy; and reject despondency, which offends God. With great trust we should look forward to Him Who said, "Take courage; it is I, do not be afraid" (Mk 6:50); Who directly summons His followers: "Take courage, I have overcome the world" (Jn 16:33). Let us repeat with Job, "Although He should kill me, I will trust in Him" (Job 13:15); for Mercy is His greatest attribute.

---

[58] At the end of this paragraph, as elsewhere in this book, Bl. Sopocko mentions in passing a Catholic theological tradition, rooted in the teachings of St. Thomas Aquinas, that whenever a soul falls into mortal sin, all the merits it had gained for all the good works it had done with the help of divine grace are thereby forfeited. However, if that soul truly repents and confesses its sins, then those merits can be fully restored by the Mercy of God. On the concept of "merit" in general in our salvation, see *Catechism*, 2006-2011.

Chapter 35

MERCY OF GOD,
ALWAYS AND EVERYWHERE
ACCOMPANYING ALL PEOPLE

*"Thy Mercy and Thy Truth
have always upheld me"*
— Psalm 39:12 [40:11]

I. Since we live in time and space, we perceive only dimensional and merely temporal objects and are unable to comprehend exactly the nature of God and His relation to time and space. Reason and faith tell us that God is fully present everywhere and at all times, past, present, and future.[59] He is omnipresent not only like the sun with its radiance on earth, or like a monarch through his power in the state, but really and indivisibly with all His essence and all His perfection. Whenever and wherever I may be, God the Father, the Son, and the Holy Spirit accompany me. The Father always perfectly comprehends Himself and begets His living image, the Son; and from the Father and the Son, through Their mutual love, the Holy Spirit proceeds. The whole Godhead with its Wisdom, Generosity, Goodness, Justice, Providence, and Mercy is always and everywhere present. "Great is the Lord, and greatly to be praised: and of his greatness there is no end" (Ps 144 [145]:3).

In some places and things, God through His Mercy is present in a more singular manner. In Heaven, God does not

---

[59] Nevertheless, as we shall see in this chapter, Bl. Sopocko also holds, along with the Catholic Tradition generally, that while God the Holy Trinity, in the fullness of His divine nature, is present everywhere in the created universe, the divine Son is present to us now in the fullness of His *humanity* (that is, in His human nature as the heavenly and glorified Jesus Christ) only in the Blessed Sacrament. See the apostolic letter of Pope St. Paul VI, *Credo of the People of God*, nos. 24-26.

conceal His Majesty, but manifests Himself to the enraptured elect in all the brightness of His throne: "We know that, when He appears, we shall be like to Him, for we shall see Him just as He is" (1 Jn 3:2).

Furthermore, God is, in a more particular manner, present in our sanctuaries, called the house of prayer in the Scriptures. Here God is, as it were, sitting on the throne of Mercy so that He might graciously hear the prayers of suppliants. Here Jesus veils His divine as well as His human brilliance so that we might approach Him as did the Samaritan woman and draw from the spring of life, which is His Heart. Here really and truly "God is with us."

Our bodies also are the temples of God: "Or do you not know that your members are the temple of the Holy Spirit" (1 Cor 6:19). In a special way God dwells in the soul of the just. "He who abides in love abides in God, and God in him" (1 Jn 4:16). In some privileged souls God is present in an extraordinary manner. He speaks to them; reveals His mysteries to them; and fills them with peace, trust, joy, and heavenly delight.

II. Although the Merciful God always and everywhere accompanies us, He does not do so in the same way in all cases. In Heaven God is visible and He acts differently there from on earth, where "no one has ever seen God" (1 Jn 4:12). He has different ways of acting in saints, in sinners, in angels, and in devils. By saying, "God descended into the souls of the just," we mean that He begins to work supernatural things in them. The saying "He withdraws Himself from the soul of the sinner" means that He ceases to act supernaturally in sinners, although He always remains in them in the natural manner as conserving their being: "He is not far from any one of us. For in Him we live and move and have our being" (Acts 17:27-28). So when we pray, "Our Father Who art in Heaven," we do not mean that He is not on earth; we mean that He acts in Heaven in a special way.

Although He is in things, God does not fuse with them, as the pantheists maintain, but remains different and distinct;

He is, at the same time, most intimately joined to them, yet most remote from them; diffused over all creation, yet most concentrated.

So we can see God in all things not only in the effects of His action and in His image but also as really remaining under the veil of created nature. On the other hand, we can see that God penetrates, maintains, and limits everything.[60] We should always be filled with the greatest joy that we have such a treasure as God Himself in our hearts, and we should always behave with due respect in the presence of the Most High. We should find time to turn our thoughts from creatures and direct them to the depths of our soul so that we might find there the immeasurable Creator.

We apply the terms "infinity" and "omnipresence" not only to the essence of God but also to His perfections (since they are not really distinct from Him), and above all else, to His Mercy. The inspired singer keeps reminding himself of the ever-present Mercy of God: "And Thy Mercy will follow me all the days of my life" (Ps 22 [23]:6).

The Blessed Virgin Mary, Mother of Mercy, also stresses, in her canticle, the universality and continuity of God's Mercy: "And His Mercy is from generation to generation" (Lk 1:50).

I will often recall to myself the Most Merciful Savior, as encompassing me on all sides, and purifying, defending, and consoling me with the graces that flow from His Sacred Heart.

---

[60] By the phrase "God ... limits everything," Bl. Sopocko may have in mind the teachings of the first chapter of the Book of Genesis in the Bible, in which God seems to set boundaries to each part of His creation (the land, the sky, the sea, etc.), and fashions every living creature according to its own natural "kind," so that to be a created being in God's world, by definition, means to have a limited, finite nature distinct from other kinds of created things — and of course, distinct from Himself as well as the one, infinite, transcendent God.

Chapter 36

MERCY OF GOD, ANTICIPATING US WITH GRACE

"Mercy and truth shall go before Thy face"
— Psalm 88:15 [89:14]

I. The world of spiritual activity has laws and forces of its own. Each person's supernatural life originates and develops in his soul in accordance with stable principles. The fundamental law and chief principle is that the primary part in our sanctification is played by God. From the very beginning the grace of God moves us to learn the premises of faith. It infuses in us the virtue of faith at Holy Baptism; it assists the soul in making acts of faith and of other virtues necessary for our salvation. So the chief cause of our sanctification is truly the Merciful God, Who arouses in us good desires, points out our last end, provides us with means for reaching it, and helps us in effectively availing ourselves of these means. For our part we have only to overcome and remove the obstacles to the operation of God's grace. That is, we have to fight against the triple concupiscence (of the flesh, of the eyes, and of the pride of life), to look to the increase of our merits through performing good acts with a pure intention, and to use reasonably the means by which we receive grace: that is, prayer and the Holy Sacraments.

"His Mercy shall prevent[61] me" (Ps 58:11 [59:10]), says the psalmist. "And Thy Mercy will follow me all the days of my life" (Ps 22 [23]:6), which means that God arouses in the soul supernatural good thoughts and desires and then helps

---

[61] The Douay-Rheims translation of the Bible here uses the archaic word "prevent" to mean "to lead the way, to take the initiative."

it to put them into effect. Now, being moved supernaturally by grace to assent to these desires, the will, in the case of sufficient grace, resists the supernatural impulse, but in that of efficacious grace it follows the impulse, performing good deeds along with the grace and under its influence. After the will has consented, the former attraction to a good does not cease, but lasts and helps the will in conforming itself to the Will of God, and thus in performing a supernaturally good act.

"But by the grace of God I am what I am, and His grace in me has not been fruitless — in fact I have labored more than any of them; yet not I, but the grace of God with me" (1 Cor 15:10), says the Apostle. Elsewhere he exhorts the faithful that they should not receive the grace of God in vain (2 Cor 6:1). Thus the grace of God attracts and leads to faith, enlightens the mind, and moves the will either indirectly, as by a sermon, or good reading, or directly by inspiring good thoughts and desires.

II. "I have planted," says St. Paul, "Apollo watered, but God has given the growth. So then neither he who plants is anything, nor he who waters, but God Who gives the growth" (1 Cor 3:6-7). For that faith to take root and increase in human hearts, it is not sufficient that priests and missionaries should preach it. Exterior graces are not sufficient; God's operation in the soul is also necessary. When Christ taught, the Jews did not accept His teaching and were indignant. Then our Savior gave the reason for their resistance, namely, that the Heavenly Father did not draw them by interior grace. "No one can come to Me unless the Father who sent Me draw him ... Everyone who has listened to the Father and has learned, comes to Me" (Jn 6:44-45). So, even the teaching of Christ was not able to draw the people to Him unless the Father also drew them by the interior anticipating grace.[62] Holy Scripture says about certain sinners that God has hardened their hearts (Ex 8:32), while the hearts of others were opened by Him (Acts 16:14).

---

[62] On the mystery of grace and free will in Bl. Sopocko's thought, and the Catholic tradition generally, see above, footnotes 53 and 54.

Thus a certain woman called Lydia believed the teaching of St. Paul in Macedonia, for God, by His interior grace, opened her heart — that is, granted her the understanding of Paul's teaching and the spirit to respond to it.

Without grace the human soul cannot, on the natural level, keep for long all the commandments of God. He cannot overcome grave temptations for a long time nor perform any supernatural act. In Holy Scripture the person without grace is compared to one in darkness (Eph 5:8), to a fool (1 Cor 2:14), to one dead (Eph 2:5), to one unborn and still not created (Jn 3:5). Grace is needed for all salutary acts: for a good thought (2 Cor 3:5), for good acts of the will (Rom 9:16), for believing and suffering for the faith (Phil 1:29), for prayer (Rom 8:26), for performing a good deed (Phil 1:6), even for saying the name of Jesus (1 Cor 12:3), but especially for beginning the life of faith and for every desire of salvation (Eph 2:8).

The grace given me by the Divine Mercy has been the prime mover for all my good acts. I will take pains never to resist God's plan for me. I will esteem highly every invitation of God, and rising I shall say immediately, "O Lord, I am ready at Your command."

COMMENTARY:
THE MERCIFUL GOD LEADS US
TO EVERLASTING LIFE

Those who follow the Way of the Cross, and put all their trust in the providential care of the Good Shepherd, move steadily forward toward life's true goal: peace of heart in this life, and peace and joy with God forever in Heaven. This theme occurs not only in Fr. Sopocko's book *God is Mercy*, but throughout his writings. As the saying goes, "The main thing is to keep the main thing the main thing." For Bl. Sopocko, this really does seem to be "the main thing." He continually pleads with us to keep in mind where true peace can be found. Thus, in an article for *Marian Helpers Bulletin* in 1956, he wrote:

> Every worldly man seeks peace and happiness without being able to find them. "Where are you hurrying, O man, on the road of life? Why do you strive for the summit so laboriously? Why all this toil, labor, and fight?" "I desire peace," answers he; "I desire to reach the goal and rest therein. I seek comfort, delight, and happiness, because man exists for these." However, instead of peace, [worldly men] find disputes, family quarrels, competition, and war of social classes and states. Why? Because they refuse to acknowledge God as their Father, and, consequently, they cannot see themselves as brothers. They feel internal discord, which nothing and no one can remove from their hearts.
>
> There are two who want to give mankind peace; the world and Christ. The peace of the world is external; the peace of Christ is internal. The former ends in confusion and collapse; the latter terminates in victory, strength, and everlasting peace.

Christ brings wonderful peace, true peace, "such as the world cannot give."[63]

Blessed Sopocko teaches that the essence of human peace and happiness consists in beholding God face to face, and loving and enjoying Him in Heaven forever. He points out that our Savior clearly promised this to us: "Blessed are the pure of heart, for they shall see God" (Mt 5:8). Likewise, when St. Paul wrote about eternal happiness, he said that it consists in the direct vision of God: "We see now [that is, in this present life] through a mirror in an obscure manner, but then [we shall see] face to face. Now I know in part, but then I shall know even as I have been known" (1 Cor 13:12). What St. Paul meant is that here on earth, our knowledge of God through faith is imperfect and only partial. As Bl. Sopocko writes: "It is merely a preparation for eternal life and eternal happiness, that is, for the perfect knowledge in which 'We shall see Him just as He is' (1 Jn 3:2)" (*God is Mercy*, chapter 39).

In this book, Bl. Sopocko sums up what the Catholic Tradition teaches about the life to come. Not surprisingly, all this coheres perfectly with what Jesus said to St. Faustina about the Heavenly Kingdom, and that she recorded in her *Diary* at the command of Fr. Sopocko:

Today I was in heaven, in spirit, and I saw its inconceivable beauties and the happiness that awaits us after death. I saw how all creatures give ceaseless praise and glory to God. I saw how great is happiness in God, which spreads to all creatures, making them happy; and then all the glory and praise which springs from this happiness returns to this source; and they enter into the depths of God, contemplating the inner life of God, the Father, the Son, and the Holy Spirit, whom they will never understand nor fathom (*Diary*, 777).

---

[63] *Marian Helpers Bulletin*, Feb 15, 1956, at https://www.thedivinemercy.org/articles/peace-and-mercy-god

> O Holy Trinity, eternal God, I thank you for allow-
> ing me to know the greatness and various degrees
> of glory to which souls attain. Oh, what a great
> difference of depth in the knowledge of God there
> is between one degree and another! Oh, if people
> could only know this! O my God, if I were thereby
> able to obtain one more degree, I would gladly
> suffer all the torments of the martyrs put together.
> Truly, all those torments seem as nothing to me
> compared with the glory that is awaiting us for all
> eternity (*Diary*, 605).

There is one aspect of Bl. Sopocko's (and St. Faustina's)
teaching about eternal life, however, that may sound strange
to Catholics today. He sometimes speaks about "meriting"
our "eternal reward," and gaining a higher place in Heaven by
our sufferings patiently borne and by our works of faith and
love. Does all this talk of merits and rewards, and climbing up
the ladder, so to speak, turn us into mercenary souls: more
concerned about what we can get for ourselves in the next life
than about loving God with all our hearts, and our neighbors
as ourselves?

Sometimes, however, offers of "rewards" are not bribes,
because they are nothing more than the invitation to bring a
certain kind of behavior to its consummation. For example,
the "reward" sought by the suitor who seeks the prize of his
beloved's hand in marriage is really only the opportunity to
go on loving her, in an ever deeper and fuller way, his whole
life long. Similarly, the "reward" Jesus offers to those who
serve Him with faith and love here on earth (see Mt 5:11,
6:19, 7:21, 16:27; see also Mt 25:31-46, Lk 12:8-9) is just the
opportunity to go on loving Him forever in Heaven, in an
ever deeper and more wonderful way. Seeking a reward like
that does not make you selfish — it just means you are a true
lover! See if there is really any selfishness in St. Alphonsus de
Liguori's matchless description of Heaven, from his meditation entitled simply "Hope":

On the instant that a soul enters heaven, and sees by the light of glory the infinite beauty of God, face to face, she is at once seized and all consumed with love. The happy soul is then as it were lost and immersed in that boundless ocean of the goodness of God. Then it is that she quite forgets herself, and inebriated with divine love, thinks only of loving her God. ... As an intoxicated person no longer thinks of himself, so the soul in bliss can only think of loving and affording delight to her beloved Lord; she desires to possess him entirely, and she does indeed possess him, for every moment she offers herself to God without reserve, and God receives her in his loving embraces, and so holds her, and shall hold her in the same fond embraces throughout eternity.[64]

---

[64] St. Alphonsus de Liguori, "The Practice of the Love of Jesus Christ," in *The Holy Eucharist* (Brooklyn: Redemptorist Fathers, 1934), pp. 442-443.

Chapter 37

MERCY OF GOD,
PEACE OF THE DYING

"Blessed are the dead who die in the Lord"
— Revelation 14:13

I. Death is the most important moment in our lives, because our eternity depends on it. For this reason, the enemy of our salvation usually assaults the souls of the dying with the greatest violence and incites them to despair. Thus the sick person is visited with thoughts full of distrust and fear that God does not have good intentions toward him; that God will let some evil fall on him; that God will not forgive these great and numerous sins that he has committed throughout his life and which now crowd his thoughts. He regards himself as only a subject of the Creator, a hireling and debtor, and forgets that he is in fact a child of his Merciful Father. Because of these thoughts the sick person usually cannot pray, and sometimes he even speaks about divine things without respect. Impatience in enduring sufferings takes hold of him, and he becomes irritable with those who surround him and feels resentment, dislike, and bitterness toward them.

He is one of those about whom St. Paul wrote: "Men will be lovers of self, covetous, haughty, proud, blasphemers, disobedient to parents, ungrateful, criminal, heartless, faithless" (2 Tim 3:2). If even the just yield to anxiety at this all-important moment, how much more anxious is the sinner who has neglected the law of God and lived in spiritual blindness? Balthasar Knelling, SJ (d. 1700), begged God for a sudden death lest he suffer the temptation of Satan in his last hour. In fact, he died at the altar after giving Holy

Communion to the faithful! Even the relatives and friends of a dying man cannot console and calm him in his last hour. This was the case with Voltaire who, prompted by horrid despair, writhed in convulsive agony. Nobody could bring him even the slightest relief.

II. The Merciful Christ has prepared a special help for this most important and dreadful moment of a person's whole life, that is, the Sacrament of Extreme Unction [i.e., Anointing of the Sick].[65] It imparts special graces to the dying man, and takes away his sins, evil inclinations, and the like. This Sacrament uplifts the spirit and confirms it in good, and even has the power to restore bodily health. In principle the Sacrament of Extreme Unction increases sanctifying grace. If, however, grave sin remains on the soul of a person who, because of physical weakness, is unable to confess his sins but on receiving Holy Oils does not resist grace, then the Sacrament of Extreme Unction operates according to its secondary effects, namely, it takes away these sins. Moreover, it effaces venial sins. The Sacrament of Extreme Unction also brings relief from temporal punishment in proportion to the good disposition of the person receiving it.

Above all else, Extreme Unction uplifts the spirit of the dying person and confirms him in good. It causes this by awakening great trust in the Mercy of God so that the sick individual suffers with patience all the inconveniences and pains that trouble him, and resists the temptations of Satan with greater fortitude. The grace proper to this Sacrament is the spiritual elevation and fortification of the dying. Under its influence the sick person is able to overcome more easily the vices acquired through repeated sins, mental blindness, and weakness of will. Thus, this Sacrament removes all remnants

---

[65] Since 1972, the Catholic Church generally refers to the Sacrament of "Extreme Unction" by one of its more ancient names, the Sacrament of "the Anointing of the Sick." One reason for the change is that this Sacrament is not reserved solely for the dying, but can be administered to anyone with a serious illness. It essentially involves prayer and an anointing with oil, both for healing of the body, and for the strengthening of faith, hope, and love in the soul.

of sin from the soul, by counteracting their pernicious influences.

So we may assert that Extreme Unction is one of the greatest works of the Mercy of God. The very form of this Sacrament points to this fact. "May the Lord, through this holy Unction and His most gracious Mercy, forgive the sins thou hast committed through sight, ... hearing, ... etc. Amen." The above prayer corresponds to the words of the Apostle: "Is any one among you sick? Let him bring in the presbyters of the Church, and let them pray over him, anointing him with oil in the name of the Lord" (Jas 5:14). It corresponds also to the condition of the sick person himself, who, deprived of his strength, cannot remove the proclivities of his sins but looks forward to help from Divine Mercy, to which he submits himself with great confidence. Hence the peaceful assurance that not only were his sins forgiven in the Sacrament of Penance, but also the remains of his sins are removed in the Sacrament of Extreme Unction.[66]

I will live so as to be ready for death at any time. I will pray for peace in the souls of those dying at this moment. I will pray that the Merciful Jesus might visit me in the hour of my death according to His great Mercy.

---

[66] By the "remains" of his sins, Bl. Sopocko seems to mean here the habits of vice that can still be present in a soul even after it has received divine pardon for sin, and the temporal punishment for sin that may still remain due to Divine Justice if the sick person's repentance for sin has been weak and halfhearted. Another effect of the "remains of sins" that is removed by Extreme Unction is the spiritual debility (i.e. spiritual weakness) and depression caused by the awareness of having sinned.

Chapter 38

MERCY OF GOD, REFRESHMENT AND RELIEF OF THE SOULS IN PURGATORY

"It is a holy and wholesome thought to pray for the dead,
that they may be loosed from sins"
— 2 Maccabees 12:46

I. Catholic teaching on Purgatory contains two dogmas: that Purgatory exists, and that it is possible to bring help to the souls remaining there. Souls in Purgatory do not advance in perfection, but suffer passively, paying the debt of the temporal punishment.[67] Theologians distinguish a twofold punishment in Purgatory: deprivation of the sight of God and punishment of the senses. Not seeing God in Purgatory differs from the similar punishment in hell, for in Purgatory the souls hope to see God, Whom they love, submitting themselves to the punishment willingly. In hell, however, despair replaces hope; hatred, blasphemy with the most intense resistance to the will of God, and punishment takes the place of love.

---

[67] Blessed Sopocko repeats here the opinion of the Thomistic tradition of theology that the soul cannot advance in sanctity after death, but it should be noted that the Catholic Church has never definitively taught this. As Catholic theologian Michael Schmaus pointed out in *Dogma 6: Justification and the Last Things* (1977, p. 244), the soul's journey through Purgatory involves an ever-deeper liberation from the prison of the self: "The soul's purification consists precisely in this process: the human 'I' is gradually pervaded by the divine love, with the effect that the person is increasingly freed of imprisonment within himself. He likewise becomes more capable of the divine self-communication." It is hard not to see this as a process of spiritual sanctification, in which the capacity of the soul to love God and receive His love is brought to fruition (see Mt 5:20; Heb 12:14). In that case, Purgatory is not only about expiating Divine Justice, but also about the healing of the soul from its spiritual defects.

Longing for the sight of God causes extreme pain to the souls in Purgatory. Saint Catherine of Genoa (d. 1510) drew the following comparison between this pain and the hunger of the body. She said that if a person did not die from hunger, because he was sustained in life by some power, nevertheless as time went on, his hunger would increase and would cause him ever greater suffering; so also the souls in Purgatory suffer more the longer their punishment continues.

The punishment of the senses in Purgatory is caused by some external object. The person while on earth had turned through sin to some external object. It is fitting, therefore, that he should be punished by it. We do not know what form this punishment takes. The Fathers of the West generally write about fire in Purgatory, and many in the East upheld the same [concept].[68]

According to St. Thomas the smallest punishment in Purgatory exceeds the greatest punishment on earth, for here the punishments have the character rather of remedy, while there the punishments consist in expiating justice.[69] As to the duration of punishment in Purgatory, one thing is certain: namely, that after the Last Judgment there will be no Purgatory. Saint Peter says about the souls at the time of the Flood (1 Pet 3:18-20) that they were not released from their prison until after the death of Christ (about 2,000 years after the Flood). From private revelations we learn that certain souls will be in Purgatory until the end of the world. The sufferings of this life often diminish in themselves or because we become accustomed to them, but in Purgatory the sufferings do not change in time. Therefore, the sufferings in Purgatory

---

[68] While Bl. Sopocko follows closely here the teaching of Aquinas that the souls in Purgatory actually suffer from *physical* fire, the Catholic Church has never defined this as a divinely revealed truth. Some Catholic theologians argue that it is improbable, since each soul in Purgatory is in a bodiless state, and will not receive a new and glorified human body until the Last Day; and some also argue that such a degree of suffering, meted out to souls in a state of grace, would be extreme and disproportionate, and therefore difficult to reconcile with Divine Love and Divine Justice. Saint Thomas explains his view in *ST App.* 1 and 2; see also his treatment of the punishment of souls in the next life in *ST Supp.* (Q. 70 and 75).

[69] See footnote 67, above.

are dreadful for three reasons: their long duration, severity, and uniformity.[70]

II. The Church's teaching on Purgatory is a manifestation of Divine Mercy, for we learn how great a difference there is between that which is due for sins according to the law of Justice, and the degree to which we can satisfy God on earth by fleeing to His Infinite Mercy. This doctrine shows the great Mercy of God for sinners. If a man has spent his whole life in sin and does not have any time left for penance, he can have the consolation that he will be able to expiate his sins after death provided he has departed from this life in the state of grace. The teaching on Purgatory gives us an opportunity to show mercy for the suffering souls and to offer Holy Masses, prayers, fasts, alms and indulgences for them, and in this manner it extends our tie of friendship and kinship beyond the grave. Moreover, this doctrine deters us from venial sins. Although a venial sin does not deprive us of our right to Heaven, yet because of it we incur a frightful punishment, for to offend God with impunity is incompatible with His Holiness and Justice. Thus, although the main reason for avoiding venial sins is that they offend God, we are also moved to avoid them because they would draw down this punishment on us. Finally, the doctrine of Purgatory stimulates us to strive for perfection, to be faithful in the smallest duties, so that after death we shall avoid punishment in purgatorial fires. Saint Ambrose, preaching a eulogy at the funeral services for Emperor Theodosius, says that he will not forget the Emperor until he would lead him, through his tears and prayers, unto the holy mountain of the Lord where there is life eternal (*P.L.* 16, 1385).

---

[70] In his encyclical *Spe Salvi*, no. 47, Pope Benedict XVI asked Catholics to be careful today when speculating on the duration of time that souls may have to spend in Purgatory. After all, the time stream there may not be the equivalent of earthly, chronological time: "It is clear that we cannot calculate the 'duration' of this transforming burning in terms of the chronological measurements of this world. The transforming 'moment' of this encounter [with Christ's love] eludes earthly time-reckoning — it is the heart's time, it is the time of 'passage' to communion with God in the Body of Christ."

The souls in Purgatory are certain of their salvation, know their own state of soul, are confirmed in good, and love the Merciful God. All this affords them great relief in their suffering. Their knowledge of the infinite Holiness of God and of their own unworthiness to behold God is great, and prompts them to bear their sufferings willingly and with utter abandonment to the Will of God, since these sufferings are the means of their purification and satisfaction for their sins. Moved by contrition, the souls in Purgatory would rather not go to Heaven than stand before God without their wedding garments. They cannot help themselves, and their only relief is God's Mercy, which awakens Christians on earth to make sacrifices for them.

> *I will not forget to pray for the souls in Purgatory and will offer my sufferings, Masses, indulgences, and good works for them. I shall remember that I myself benefit the most by such acts, since the souls in Purgatory gain from them remission of punishment only, whereas I, at the same time, would obtain remission of guilt and punishment for my sins as well as grace and fervor in acquiring virtue.*

Chapter 39

MERCY OF GOD, HEAVENLY DELIGHT OF THE BLESSED

"I am thy reward exceeding great"
— Genesis 15:1

I. Humanity's earthly environment is the background against which we develop our faculties and perfect our physical and spiritual being. Only when we die will the depth of eternal life, in which God is the reward of the elect, their joy, and their happiness, be unveiled to us. Revelation alone tells us something about this happiness.

First of all, the happiness of the elect will be supernatural; that is, it will exceed all the powers and needs of rational creatures and will be attained only by supernatural means. Such happiness may be essential or accidental. (Accidental happiness will be dealt with in the following chapter 40.)

Essential happiness consists in beholding God face to face, loving Him and enjoying Him. Our Savior promised this to us. "They are as Angels of God in heaven" (Mt 22:30) who regard the face of the Father. "Blessed are the pure of heart, for they shall see God" (Mt 5:8). Likewise, St. Paul, when speaking of eternal happiness, says that it consists in our vision of God. "We see now through a mirror in an obscure manner, but then [we shall see] face to face. Now I know in part, but then I shall know even as I have been known" (1 Cor 13:12). Also Christ, in His prayer as the High Priest, says, "Now this is everlasting life, that they may know Thee, the only true God" (Jn 17:3). Here on earth, our knowledge of God through faith is imperfect and merely partial. It is a preparation for eternal

life and eternal happiness, that is, for the perfect knowledge
in which "We shall see Him just as He is" (1 Jn 3:2).

Apart from seeing God, another factor that makes for
the happiness of the saints is their love of God. "So there abide
faith, hope, and charity, these three; but the greatest of these
is charity; charity never fails" (1 Cor 13:13 and 8). The [true
fulfilment] of our will is love, and the object of love is the
good. It is impossible for the soul to see God, the Supreme
Good, without loving Him with the most fervent love. Now,
love brings happiness, so the love of God causes the greatest
happiness for the saints in Heaven.

II. How will this vision and love of God be brought about?
Through the very special Mercy of God. So great is the
inequality between God, the infinite Being, and humanity, as
finite beings, that the future vision of God seems to be mere
fiction. But the promises of God do not fail. Since God has
called us to know and love Him, we must believe that He will
enable us to attain this, though it surpasses all our powers.
If God created natural light, which impinges on the eye and
enables us to know remote objects, what is there to prevent
Him from enabling us to know the Infinite? For human
beings to see God, their nature must be transformed, and this
process is already started on earth by grace, through which
Divine Life pours into our soul. After death, this life will be
perfected in "the light of glory," in which the Supreme Being
will become, as it were, a form for our reason.[71] Through this,
God will manifest Himself to us and unite with our nature as
the sun unites with our eyes, and we shall lift our countenance
to the radiant face of the Godhead. Although miraculously
transformed and perfected through its union with God in
"the light of Glory," the human soul will remain finite and
will not be able to know God completely. God alone knows
Himself perfectly. However, for a finite nature it is sufficient

---

[71] Here again, Bl. Sopocko uses the word "form," derived from the philosopher
Aristotle, to indicate that in the beatific vision, the human faculty of reason is, as it
were, re-formed to enable it to behold the essence of God.

to know and to love as much as it has merited to know and love. God, the Supreme Beauty, of which the earthly marvels are only a weak reflection, will enrapture the soul and bring it an ineffable joy. "And your heart shall rejoice, and your joy no one shall take from you" (Jn 16:22). Vision, love, and sublime enjoyment of God will be the essential delight of the blessed for eternity. This delight is not due nor merited by the saints on the scales of Divine Justice, but is given to them through the infinite Mercy of God. As the psalmist says, "The mercies of the Lord I will sing for ever" (Ps 88 [89]:1).

I long for the happiness, for the delight of the blessed. I trust that God will receive me into their midst, and that the Mercy of God will be the light and joy of my soul in eternity because I venerate it here and now.

Chapter 40

MERCY OF GOD,
CROWN OF ALL SAINTS

"Who crowneth thee with Mercy and compassion"
— Psalm 102 [103]:4

I. In Holy Scripture eternal happiness is often called the crown. "For the rest, there is laid up for me a crown of justice, which the Lord, the just Judge, will give to me in that day" (2 Tim 4:8). Saint John saw in a vision the saints in Heaven with golden crowns: "and upon the seats twenty-four elders sitting, clothed in white garments, and on their heads crowns of gold" (Rev 4:4). These crowns symbolize that our accidental happiness is the uncreated Good, God Himself. Accidental happiness, common to all saints, flows from the good of the soul and of the body and from external goods.[72]

In Heaven, affirms Suárez, the memory of what was done on earth will be preserved. Moreover, the soul will possess infused knowledge through which it will know the glorified human nature of Christ, the properties of His Soul and of His glorified Body. This will result in untold happiness for it. The soul will also know the Queen of Heaven and earth, the holy

---

[72] Blessed Sopocko's language here is ambiguous. What is "accidental" to an existing thing is something that is not essential to its nature, such as quantity (e.g., whether I am fat or skinny), quality (whether I am a skilled musician or a chimney sweep), or relationships (whether I am married or single, live in North America or Asia, etc.). I am essentially a human being no matter what may be true of me in any of these "accidental" ways. Here Bl. Sopocko says that our *accidental* happiness is God in His goodness — but, arguably, there is a sense in which God Himself is our *essential* beatitude as well, since He has made us spiritual and rational creatures. In other words, unlike turnips and jellyfish, we can be elevated by grace to a supernatural, eternal state and receive the beatific vision. Accidental happiness from God would seem to consist more in some of His other benefits, such as consolations in prayer and the freedom from all possibility of suffering in our heavenly body.

angels, and the souls of other saints. Finally, it will know, of all the works of the universe and of the whole history of the earth, all that is of interest to it and all that it should know.[73]

As to their will, the saints will have no sorrow either for their own sins for which they did penance, or for the sins of others, since they will realize that the Mercy of God has turned everything to good, and that even the condemned, though unwilling, give honor to God and find themselves under the operation of His Justice, since on earth they had shunned the worship due to the Merciful God.[74]

The reunion of the soul and the body will increase the joy of the soul on the day of the resurrection because of the glorious attributes that will adorn the body: *impassibility,* freedom from any suffering; *clarity,* positive radiance, as well as freedom from shame and from animal functions; *agility,* the ability to move merely by willing to do so; and *subtlety,* the ability to pass through other material objects without affecting them.

---

[73] By this phrase, "all that is of interest to [the soul], and all that it should know," Bl. Sopocko may be referring to the common opinion of Catholic theologians that God grants each person in Heaven the knowledge of all that pertained to his earthly life, and to his role in the heavenly Kingdom, but this does not mean that each person will know "everything." For example, it is doubtful that many souls in Heaven need to know all the physics involved in space travel, or all the details of molecular biology.

[74] According to a venerable Catholic tradition, the Immaculate Heart of Mary in Heaven is pierced by the sins, sufferings, and sorrows of human beings on earth (manifest symbolically in reported cases of statues of Mary actually shedding tears). Theologians have often sought to explain the matter this way: The glorified human nature of Jesus, of the Blessed Virgin, and of the saints in Heaven, enjoying forever the beatific vision of the eternal radiance of God, is "impassible" (that is, beyond all "suffering," in the literal sense of the word), but not "insensible" to human sin and sorrow as these still occur on earth. If in Heaven they cannot suffer literally from "grief" or "sadness" any longer (for if they could, the triumph of Easter would be compromised), nevertheless, they are still capable of receiving additional, "accidental" joy whenever they see the conversion and sanctification of human souls, and the relief of human suffering and misery (on the meaning of "accidental" in the Catholic tradition, see note 72 above). This kind of heavenly joy, however, often is denied to them by souls on earth who stubbornly refuse to repent, or by the temporary ascendency in human history of cruelty, oppression, sickness, and suffering. Thus, their heavenly longing, flowing from their merciful love for the good of each and every person on earth is not always fulfilled, and in that sense the hearts of Jesus, Mary, and the saints may be said to be affected with something analogous to human, earthly sorrow.

As for external created goods, association with Christ, His Mother, His angels, and His saints will be a particular joy for the blessed. The happiness of some will be the cause of joy for others and the love of God will unite all the saints into one Mystical Body, the Head of which is the most Merciful Christ.

II. Distinct from accidental happiness, common to all saints, there is a happiness proper to certain saints only. Venerable Bede (d. 735) calls particular happiness a crown of gold (*corona aureola*), and St. Thomas calls it a privileged reward corresponding to a privileged victory. The Angelic Doctor defines the aureole as "a certain joy flowing from these deeds of the saints which have the mark of outstanding victory" (Suppl. 96, 1). Martyrs, Doctors, and virgins will have this kind of aureole.

The blessed virgins have won a splendid victory over bodily passions; St. John tells us in the Apocalypse about their particular happiness and distinction. "And they were singing as it were a new song before the throne, and before the four living creatures and the elders; and no one could learn the song except these hundred and forty-four thousand, who have been purchased from the earth" (Rev 14:3). The blessed martyrs have gained their distinction for their victory over the persecutors of the Church. Saint John says of the martyrs: "These (clothed in white robes) are they who have come out of the great tribulation, and have washed their robes and made them white in the blood of the Lamb" (Rev 7:14). The prophets, that is, apostles and writers of the Church, spread the Kingdom of God on earth. "But they that are learned shall shine as the brightness of the firmament: and they that instruct many to justice, as stars for all eternity" (Dan 12:3). The aureole is a special glory of the soul. However, after the soul joins the body, the joy flowing from special deeds will manifest itself also in the body. "Eye has not seen ... what things God has prepared for those who love him" (1 Cor 2:9).

Our Lord, before His Passion, asked the Father "that they may be perfected in unity" (Jn 17:23). So in spite of the difference in their degrees of glory, the saints in Heaven will constitute a harmonious unity. It will be one eternal song of adoration, love, and gratitude for the infinite Mercy of God which is the crown of all saints. "Mercy shall be built up for ever in the heavens" (Ps 88:3 [89:2]).

Great intimacy reigns among the saints and their crown is the Humanity of Christ. I will surround the Blessed Sacrament with the greatest reverence since it contains this Humanity through which I may gain admission to the communion of saints.

Chapter 41

MERCY OF GOD, INEXHAUSTIBLE SOURCE OF MIRACLES

"Now by the hands of the apostles many signs and wonders were done"

— Acts 5:12

I. A miracle is an extraordinary fact, perceptible to the senses, that exceeds all powers of nature and can be produced solely by God. Since God is the Author of the laws of nature, He can sustain their operation or produce something that goes beyond the laws established by Himself. Such an act does not change the Will of God, for the act was foreseen and decreed by the Divine Will from all eternity.

Miracles are, as it were, a seal of God impressed on revealed truth. They are God's signature to show that He acknowledges a certain teaching as His own. Since God is all holy, He could not put His signature and seal to a lie. Therefore, if someone teaches a doctrine, as revealed by God, and performs miracles in confirmation of this doctrine, the teaching is certainly revealed. Although false religions also claim the existence of miracles within their history, unlike the Catholic Church they are not in a position to prove their authenticity.[75]

---

[75] Here, it would seem at first that Bl. Sopocko has overstated the case for the probative value of miracles. After all, Jesus predicts that false Christs and false prophets will "show signs and wonders, so as to lead astray, if possible, even the elect" (Mt 24:24), and St. Paul warns us of the deceptive powers of the Antichrist: "The coming of the lawless one by the activity of Satan will be with all power and with pretended signs and wonders, and with all wicked deception" (2 Thess 2:9-10). Demonic forces, therefore, would seem to have the power to perform miracles

Scripture relates many miracles wrought by the patri-
archs and prophets by Divine Power. Thus, Moses led the
Israelites through the Red Sea, later produced water out of a
rock, and for 40 years caused manna and quail to fall onto the
earth. Elias brought fire down onto the earth, and multiplied
flour and oil. Elisha cured the sick and raised the dead.

The greatest number of miracles were wrought by our
Lord during His earthly life. He Himself said to the disciples
of John the Baptist, "Go and report to John what you have
heard and seen: the blind see, the lame walk, the lepers
are cleansed, the deaf hear, the dead rise" (Mt 11:4-5). The
glorious Resurrection was the greatest miracle of our Lord,
regarding which St. Paul says: "And if Christ has not risen,
vain is your faith" (1 Cor 15:17). Our Savior continues to work

---

in order to trick people into believing falsehoods, and into following false leaders
and teachers. This reportedly happens at times to those who practice wicca, magic,
or the occult. All this is one reason why, when the Church investigates a claim of
extraordinary private or prophetic revelations (e.g., those received by St. Faustina),
she does not just judge the case on evidence of accompanying miracles, but also (1)
on the presence of sanity and virtue in the alleged recipient of those special revelations, (2) on the fruit the revelations seem to bear in the Christian community (e.g.,
conversions, increased love for our Lord, and recourse to the Sacraments), and (3) on
the compatibility between the alleged revelations and the public revelation already
given to the world through Christ and His apostles, as found in Holy Scripture and
Sacred Tradition, and defined by the Church's Magisterium. In short, if we are using
the word "miracles" in the way the word is used in common parlance today — that
is, as the act of an immaterial (and in that sense "supernatural") power that cannot be
produced by the material creation on its own — then such "miracles," by themselves,
are not sufficient evidence that it is God Who is truly at work, rather than some
other natural or supernatural agent (such as an angel or a demon). Also, it would
not be impossible for God to bless the work of a wise and virtuous non-Christian
prophet or sage with a gift of healing or prophecy, for providential reasons known
only to Himself. For example, there are many miracles reported in response to the
prayers of devout Jewish rabbis down through history, but such miracles alone do
not raise all the teachings of those rabbis to the rank of divine revelation.

Blessed Sopocko certainly was well aware of all this, since he undertook an
investigation into the authenticity of Sr. Faustina's revelations himself, and he did
not base that discernment solely on evidence of the miraculous in her life. Moreover,
if we look at the definition he offered of "miracle" at the start of this chapter, he was
careful to define that a miracle is something that "exceeds all the powers of nature,"
and therefore "can only be performed by God." On this definition of "miracle," a
demonic agent, as a created being, possesses extraordinary, but not "supernatural"
power (in the Catholic tradition, angelic or demonic power is sometimes called
"preternatural" power). On this reckoning, therefore, the only truly "supernatural"
power would be God Himself.

miracles in His saints. However, the continued existence and growth of the Church despite all adversities for so many ages are truly His greatest miracles since the Resurrection.

II. The infinite Mercy of God is the source of all miracles. Just as all graces come from God, so also all miracles under the Old Testament were performed by the power of the eternal Word. "All things were made through Him, and without Him was made nothing that has been made" (Jn 1:3).

Under the New Testament the Savior Himself, or the apostles in His Name, wrought miracles (Acts 9:34ff); His servants have performed and still perform them in the Catholic Church to this day. From the year 1858, miracles have been performed in Lourdes through the mediation of the Blessed Virgin Mary, but their Author is her Son, the God-Man. "All things were made through Him" (Jn 1:3).

Christ might have performed no miracles at all, yet all the world could be at His feet. Or He might have wrought thousands of the greatest miracles, yet instead of attracting souls He would repel and terrify them, if He did not show moral beauty, sweetness, benignity, and mercy in performing those miracles. He had dreadful power in His hand, yet He used it not to punish the arrogant Pharisees but only to show Mercy to human wretchedness. No sooner did He meet the poor or sick than He hastened to help them; on such occasions He even trembled and was filled with emotion, a sign of His great compassion. With what tenderness He raised the son of the widow of Nain. With what pity He took the hand of the daughter of Jairus and said to her, "*Talitha cumi!*" — "Girl, arise!" (Mk 5:41; Lk 8:54). With what emotion did He raise Lazarus. But why no miracle before Herod? Why no miraculous descent from the Cross when the Pharisees on Golgotha asked for it? Because it would be not a deed of Mercy and pity toward human misery, but a mere satisfaction of the sinful curiosity of unbelievers.

The purpose and application of miracles, and not the mere fact of their performance, give testimony to the Mercy of our Savior. Christ's restraint and mastery in using this power are the crown of His perfection, a moral miracle surpassing all physical miracles. Truly the Mercy of God is an inexhaustible source of miracles.

I believe in the miracle performed each day in the Holy Mass. It is a continuous and miraculous multiplication of the angelic bread and pouring of graces on the zealous and on the lukewarm souls. I desire to expand my love and prepare myself for an ever more fruitful reception of this inexhaustible source of miracles.

Chapter 42

LAMB OF GOD,
THE KING OF MERCY

"Behold the Lamb of God,
Who takes away the sin of the world!"
— John 1:29

I. John the Baptist announced the coming of the Savior in the words "Behold the lamb of God." It is characteristic of a lamb to let itself be led wherever the shepherd wants, to let itself be offered as a sacrifice. For us Jesus is a Shepherd: "I am the good shepherd" (Jn 10:11). For the Heavenly Father He is a Lamb. The first movement of His Heart was to offer Himself as a sacrifice for the sins of the world. Therefore, on entering the world He said, "Sacrifice and oblation Thou wouldst not, but a body Thou hast fitted to me: in holocausts, and sin-offerings Thou hast had no pleasure. Then said I, 'Behold I come' — (in the head of the book it is written of Me) — 'to do Thy will, O God'" (Heb 10:5-7). Christ never went back on this commitment. "I do not resist: I have not gone back. I have given My body to the strikers, and My cheeks to them that plucked them: I have not turned away My face from them that rebuked Me" (Is 50:5-6). Dying on the Cross, He cried, "It is consummated! ... Father, into Thy hands I commend My spirit" (Jn 19:30; Lk 23:46).

The Lamb of God is our Shepherd and our King, the King of Mercy. He established an eternal kingdom, which is not of this world (Jn 18:36), but which dwells in the souls of the just. It comprises all the faithful on earth (the Church militant), the saints in Heaven (the Church triumphant), and the souls in Purgatory (the Church suffering). In this Kingdom the Lamb of God is the King and its foundation is Mercy. It was Christ's mission on earth to unveil the mystery of Mercy to souls. It is not opportune here to elaborate the proofs for this. So that we may have a better idea of the King of Mercy, let it suffice to mention Jesus' parables of the Good Shepherd, of the Prodigal Son, and of the lost drachma, or such figures as Mary Magdalen, the woman taken in adultery, Peter the Apostle, and the thief on the cross.

The Lamb of God is always the King of Mercy. Not only did He redeem the world once and for all by His death on the Cross, but He continually renews His sacrifice in every Holy Mass in an unbloody manner. In the name of all humanity He offers the homage of adoration and of thanksgiving to the Heavenly Father for all the merciful graces we receive, and entreats for His adopted brethren the effusion of new graces, the greatest of which is the grace of forgiveness.

II. "I have come to cast fire upon the earth, and what will I but that it be kindled?" (Lk 12:49), said the Lamb of God to His contemporaries. Today He repeats the same words to us. Each Christian should strive to be aflame with this fire but first of all those to whom Christ confided His mysteries, whom He called his friends and spouses, who by their vocation are called to spread the Kingdom of God. We cannot remain lukewarm in this work. We have to be aflame with the fire of zeal visible even in our external activity. Zeal is the flame of love or of hatred. The enemies of Christ are incited by hatred; we should be urged by love. Otherwise, we shall be vomited out of the mouth of the Lamb of God (Rev 3:16), that is, eliminated from the number of His servants.

Our zeal should be known by the respect we bear toward those with whom we associate (even though they be our enemies); through patience and meekness in imitation of the Lamb, Who said, "Learn from Me, for I am meek and humble of heart" (Mt 11:29); by rendering services to the needy and especially by performing works of mercy for the soul and body of our neighbor; and through our personal sanctification, without which we cannot bring about the sanctification and conversion of others. Also, we shall never attain perfection nor unite ourselves with the Lamb of God and the King of Mercy unless we receive that portion of the chalice which our Lord ordained for us to drink with Him and in imitation of Him. Let us benefit from the examples of Fr. Maximilian Kolbe[76] and many others who have shown outstanding virtue in our times.

In days of sorrow, sickness, temptation, and spiritual dryness; in hours of trials and distress, however painful they may be, I will turn to the Lamb of God and commend to Him my affliction, the cross appointed to me by His Mercy. I will follow the way that the Lamb of God taught St. Mechtilde: "If someone wills to offer Me a pleasant sacrifice, let him flee to Me in his affliction and complain to no one; let him give himself to Me with confidence and entrust to Me the anxieties of his heart. I will not abandon him who does so."

---

[76] [From the 1965 edition] Father Maximilian Kolbe was a Polish Franciscan who was sent by the Nazis to the infamous concentration camp in Auschwitz in May 1941. By the end of July, one of the prisoners managed to escape from the camp. At the roll call of the prisoners, in reprisal for this escape, 10 prisoners were chosen by the commandant of the camp for starvation to death. To save one of his fellow prisoners, Fr. Kolbe willingly offered himself to suffer death in his stead. After 10 days of lack of food and water, Fr. Kolbe, still alive, was killed by an injection of carbolic acid. He died on August 14, the eve of the Feast of the Assumption of Our Lady. [New text of this footnote, added in 2022] He was canonized on October 10, 1982, by Pope St. John Paul II. Blessed Sopocko revered Fr. Kolbe, and in his personal diary lamented the fact that he himself had not yet attained the virtue of courage manifested by this saint of Auschwitz:

> I really admired the life of Fr. Maximilian Kolbe. I admired his dedica-
> tion to the faith and his heroism in terrible conditions. ... I have carried
> out acts of bravery in my life, but fear always stopped me short at some
> point. I feel I could have done great things, but in the end, unlike Fr.
> Kolbe, I had not the courage to do them (*The Memoirs of Blessed Fr.
> Michael Sopocko*, Divine Mercy Publications edition, 2017, p. 255).

These words were written by Fr. Sopocko before he was given by God the role of spiritual director to St. Faustina, and chief propagator of the Divine Mercy message and devotion — tasks in which he would be called to embrace much suffering. In the end, it seems, he did attain the virtue of courage that he so longed for, and he did indeed do "great things" for Christ and His Church.

Chapter 43

THE WILL OF GOD
AND THE MERCY OF GOD

"Father, ...
not My will but Thine be done"
— Luke 22:42

I. The power by which an intelligent being seeks the good that is suitable for him is called the will. Human beings, angels, and God possess it. Divine Will differs from the will of other intelligent beings in that God does not strive for the possession of any exterior good, as He already possesses in Himself the good in all its fullness, and He loves and enjoys it. God observes a proper order in the objects of His Will. In the first place He loves that which is most worthy of His love: namely, His Goodness, which is the cause of goodness in all creatures. The secondary objects of the Divine Will are His creatures in which He loves His Goodness.[77] However, this love of God for creatures is, properly speaking, His Mercy, as we saw in chapter 8.

God rejoices in intelligent creatures and in their good works: "My delights were to be with the children of men" (Prov 8:31). God desires only happiness for intelligent creatures; therefore, the Divine Will is in relation to us full of Kindness, Generosity, Providence, Justice, and above all else Mercy. "Thy Mercy and Thy Truth have always upheld me" (Ps 39:12 [40:11]), cries the psalmist who was rescued from many dangers.

---

[77] In other words, He loves His creatures because they are products of His Goodness as their Creator, and can manifest His Goodness in a myriad of ways.

The Will of God is partly known to us and partly hidden. Jesus made the Divine Will known to us, and God twice (at the Jordan and on Mount Tabor) commanded us to obey Him. "This is My beloved Son, in Whom I am well pleased, hear Him" (Mt 17:5). On the other hand, the Son said that He would make us know everything that the Father asked Him to reveal. "All things that I have heard from My Father I have made known to you" (Jn 15:15). So Scripture, Tradition, the Church, and the voice of our superiors are the Will of God expressly revealed to us, which as a gift of Mercy we should esteem highly, love, and fulfill.[78] The psalmist says, "My eyes are ever towards the Lord" (Ps 24 [25]:15), in order that he may watch and fulfill the Will of God. Thus our Savior acted: "I do always the things that are pleasing to Him" (Jn 8:29).

The hidden Will of God covers the whole of our natural and supernatural life: our health, our actual situation, our success and failure, the hour and circumstances of our death, and the degree of our sanctity and the means leading to it — all this is unknown and hidden from us. The attitude of the soul to the Will of God is twofold: it can guide itself by the natural light of reason [alone] and proceed according to its own will, or it can surrender itself to the Will of God entirely and in all things. The former case involves the wisdom of this world, which, in the words of St. Paul, is "foolishness with God" (1 Cor 3:19). We must not guide ourselves by such wisdom: "For My thoughts are not your thoughts: nor your ways My ways, saith the Lord" (Is 55:8).

II. "Blessed are the poor in spirit ... the meek ... they who mourn ... the merciful ... the clean of heart ... they who suffer persecution." These and many others are the Divine Ideals, which are proposed to us on every page of the Gospel. Facing these plans and designs of God toward us we should assume an

---

[78] Blessed Sopocko does not mean that these expressions of the Divine Will should be obeyed with equal dedication. Clearly, what God has revealed to be true about His Will through Holy Scripture and Sacred Tradition should take precedence over any fallible decrees issued by Church authorities, or issued by our ecclesiastical and secular "superiors."

attitude of complete surrender to the Will of God, of placing our personality and all our opinions in the hands of the most Merciful Lord so that we might accept the decrees of God with all humility as our Savior did in the Garden of Olives. True wisdom is not to have one's own will in these things but to trust the infallible Word of God, His eternal Wisdom, and His infinite Mercy.

In our surrender to the Will of God we give the Divine Mercy a continuous homage of faith (Abraham), of hope (David), and of love (the Blessed Virgin Mary). God conducts Himself toward us as we do towards Him. He measures out His Mercy to us according to our attitude toward Him. The more we give ourselves to Him, the more His Mercy enters into the details and circumstances of our life. The more we consider Him as our Father, the more He shows His tender regard for us, for He is ever watching over us. No mother was ever so solicitous for her infant, no friend ever consoled his friends as God does when He encompasses with solicitude and consoles the soul that gives itself to Him. It suffices to approach such a soul to feel the all-sweet unction flowing from its immovable trust in Divine Mercy and from the union with God that results from this trust. Consent to the Will of God in all things — this is the straightest and shortest way to sanctity.

At present, many things are hidden from me. I do not know whether I shall live long, what health I shall enjoy, whether God will lead me to Himself this or another way. Concerning all this I will preserve the greatest calm. Even in the worst situations I will adore the Wisdom and Omnipotence of God and cast myself into the embrace of Divine Mercy as a child seeks the arms of its mother, and I will go wherever He wills to lead me. "Can a woman forget her infant, so as not to have pity on the son of her womb? And if she should forget, yet will not I forget thee" (Is 49:15).

I know that God wills my sanctity, and that He acts for this end, and that He possesses a thousand means to bring it about. Joys and sorrows, light and darkness, consolation and dryness, health and sickness — all this is for my salvation. So I will follow Your advice, O Merciful Savior, which You gave to St. Gertrude: "Make an act of giving yourself to My good pleasure that I may freely dispose of everything concerning you. ... In all unite your sentiments with the sentiments of My most merciful Heart!"

Join the

Association of Marian Helpers,

headquartered at the National Shrine of The Divine Mercy, and share in special blessings!

An invitation from
Fr. Joseph, MIC, director

Marian Helpers is an Association of Christian faithful of the Congregation of Marian Fathers of the Immaculate Conception. By becoming a member, you share in the spiritual benefits of the daily Masses, prayers, and good works of the Marian priests and brothers.

This is a special offer of grace given to you by the Church through the Marian Fathers. Please consider this opportunity to share in these blessings, along with others whom you would wish to join into this spiritual communion.

1-800-462-7426 • Marian.org/join

Spiritual Enrollments & Masses

Enroll your loved ones in the Association of Marian Helpers, and they will participate in the graces from the daily Masses, prayers, good works, and merits of the Marian priests and brothers around the world.

Request a Mass to be offered by the Marian Fathers for your loved ones

Individual Masses
(for the living or deceased)

Gregorian Masses
(30 days of consecutive Masses for the deceased)

1-800-462-7426 • Marian.org/enrollments • Marian.org/mass

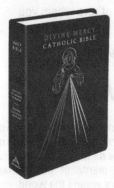
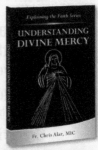